User Surveys in College Libraries

CLIP Note #23

Compiled by

Mignon S. Adams
Director of Library Services
Philadelphia College of Pharmacy and Science
Philadelphia, Pennsylvania

Jeffrey A. Beck
Reference and Electronic Resources Librarian
Wabash College
Crawfordsville, Indiana

College Library Information Packet Committee
College Libraries Section
Association of College and Research Libraries
A Division of the American Library Association

ASSOCIATION OF

COLLEGE

& RESEARCH

LIBRARIES

A DIVISION OF THE
AMERICAN LIBRARY ASSOCIATION

Published by the Association of College and Research Libraries
A Division of the American Library Association
50 East Huron Street
Chicago, IL 60611
1-800-545-2433

ISBN 0-8389-7813-4

Printed on recycled paper.

Printed in the United States of America.

TABLE OF CONTENTS

INTRODUCTION   1

SELECTED BIBLIOGRAPHY   7

CLIP NOTES SURVEY RESULTS   9

USER SURVEYS

General Surveys

Eckerd College Library   18
St. Petersburg, FL

Julia Rogers Library   19
Goucher College
Baltimore, MD

Bradley University Library   25
Peoria, IL

Farrell Family Library   26
Trinity College of Vermont
Burlington, VT

Williams College Library   27
Williamstown, MA

Surveys Adapted from Other Sources

American Library Association Survey   34

St. Florence Library   35
Our Lady of the Lake University
San Antonio, TX

Measuring Academic Library Performance Survey (ALA, 1990)   36

Arkansas Tech University Library   38
Russellville, AR

Transylvania University Library   39
Lexington, KY

Surveys of Online Services

Drew University Library
Madison, NJ
42

Peterson Memorial Library
Walla Walla College
College Place, WA
46

Feinberg Library
State University of New York
Plattsburgh, NY
47

Surveys on Specific Areas of the Library

St. Olaf Libraries
St. Olaf College
Northfield, MN
50

Simpson Library
Mary Washington College
Fredericksburg, VA
52

Lavery Library
St. John Fisher College
Rochester, NY
55

Facilities Surveys

Cochran Library
Sweet Briar College
Sweet Briar, VA
60

Jesse Ball duPont Library
University of the South
Sewanee, TN
64

Focus Groups and Interviews

L. A. Beeghly Library
Ohio Wesleyan University
Delaware, OH
66

Wheelock College Library   76
Wheelock College
Boston, MA

Sarah Byrd Askew Library   83
William Paterson College
Wayne, NJ

Reports

John F. Kennedy Library   94
Eastern Washington University
Cheney, WA

Marist College Library   99
Poughkeepsie, NY

Meader Library   101
Hawaii Pacific University
Honolulu, HI

Accompanying Documents

Cochran Library   106
Sweet Briar College
Sweet Briar, VA

J. W. England Library   107
Philadelphia College of Pharmacy and Science
Philadelphia, PA

Transylvania University Library   108
Lexington, KY

Gardner-Webb University Library   110
Boiling Springs, NC

Carl B. Ylvisaker Library   111
Concordia College
Moorhead, MN

INTRODUCTION

Objective

In 1980, the College Library Section of the Association of College and Research Libraries began the *College Library Information Packet (CLIP) Notes Series* so that college and small university libraries could share with each other the documents and policies that they have created. This *CLIP Note* provides examples of user surveys and supporting documents that have been developed by college librarians to obtain feedback from the clientele they serve.

Background

Americans are no strangers to surveys. They fill out census forms every ten years, respond to political opinion pollsters during every election period, and are contacted regularly by market researchers. In addition to professional surveys, many organizations conduct their own surveys without following standardized procedures.

Survey research as a field of study began with the U. S. Census. Techniques developed by those who designed the Census were honed by others. Market researchers wanted to determine reactions to possible products. Politicians wanted to know voters' preferences before election day. Social scientists wanted to ascertain social beliefs and attitudes. By the 1950's, these researchers had determined the basic principles of designing and analyzing surveys. Accepted principles of sampling, questionnaire wording, and analysis of responses have not changed in forty years.

Two new methods of surveying--the telephone interview and the focus group--have emerged in the last twenty-five years. Until then, the greater cost of face-to-face interviews had meant that mailed surveys were more common, even though the use of skilled interviewers produces higher rates of return and more accurate responses. When randomized telephone dialing became possible in the early 1970's, telephone interviews became the most cost-effective way to reach large numbers of respondents.

People often act in an opposite way from the responses they give to surveys. For example, citizens may express support for one candidate then vote for another. In the late 1970's, market researchers began to use focus groups, small groups of eight to ten people gathered together to discuss predetermined topics under the direction of a trained facilitator. Focus groups yield rich information and appear to be more effective than either surveys or interviews in drawing out an individual's true feelings and opinions. However, social science researchers caution that focus groups are not appropriate for generating statistics or formulating generalizations. Focus groups are not representative enough to be used as random sampling can be.

All three approaches--self-administered surveys, interviews and focus groups--are currently in use. Surveys are an economical method to reach a large number of people, particularly if there are ways to ensure a high rate of response (as, for example, administering the survey in a classroom). Interviews are a fairly easy way to obtain in-depth information. Focus groups are especially useful in understanding why particular programs succeed or fail, or in identifying issues that may subsequently be used in a survey.

Library Surveys

As indicated by the response to this *Clip Note*, librarians at the majority of college libraries use surveys. Surveys offer an opportunity to provide administrators and accrediting agencies with documentation about what users think about library services, facilities, and collections; give feedback in order to make better decisions; and identify the priorities of the library clientele.

The response to this *Clip Note* also indicates that the most common instrument developed in college libraries is the self-administered user satisfaction survey. Such surveys are aimed at measuring whether or not users find a whole array of services satisfactory and are often developed as part of a self-study for accreditation purposes. Survey researchers would likely discourage a survey like this as too unfocused and unlikely to yield enough information to make decisions. However, college librarians have conducted user satisfaction surveys to identify problem areas and to take a "snapshot" for comparison over the years.

By the 1980's, accrediting agencies began to ask for performance or output measures as evidence that institutional goals were being met. In response, the Association of College and Research Libraries set up a task force in 1985 charged with overseeing the development of performance measures for academic libraries. *Measuring Academic Library Performance*, by Nancy Van House, Beth Weil, and Charles McClure (ALA, 1990) was written as a result of the efforts of the task force. It includes several survey instruments and directions for determining a number of different library outcomes. Many libraries have used these instruments, as well as a quick "customer satisfaction survey" developed by the American Library Association in 1994.

Interviews appear to be much less used in college libraries than self-administered surveys. Perhaps college librarians obtain an adequate response rate with mailed or distributed questionnaires. However, college librarians have begun to use focus groups, often utilizing expertise on their campuses to plan and conduct the groups. Focus groups have been used to explore issues such as how students actually conduct research, with findings that should impact on the content of library instruction. Focus groups have also been used as a preliminary tool to identify matters of concern to faculty or students so that a written survey can be developed based on these issues.

This *CLIP Note* contains a wide variety of survey instruments used in college libraries. Included are general user satisfaction surveys, surveys concerned with one area or aspect of the library, and adaptations of the forms from Van House and the American Library Association. There are several scripts for focus groups and interviews. Since other kinds of materials can make a difference in a survey's response rate, examples of cover letters, directions, and rewards for completed surveys are also included. Finally, there are examples of reports which discuss survey findings and decisions based on those findings.

Survey Procedures

The survey was conducted according to the standard procedures used for *CLIP Notes*. The two co-authors determined and refined the objectives of the survey and developed a planning grid and a preliminary draft. Questions were piloted by telephone interviews with six library directors who had conducted user surveys.

Following revision and approval by the ACRL/College Library Section Committee on *CLIP Notes*, surveys were mailed in April, 1995 to the 265 college and small university library directors who have agreed to participate in *CLIP Notes* surveys. An address label was enclosed with the survey. There were 185 responses to the first mailing, and those not responding received a follow-up letter. The final response totalled 214.

ANALYSIS OF SURVEY RESULTS

The significance and interest in this topic is illustrated by the eighty-one percent response rate (214 responses) to the survey questionnaire. A complete presentation of the results of the survey follows this brief summ'ry that highlights the key findings.

Institution Profile and Participation (Questions 1-4, 19)

Institutions agreeing to participate in the CLIP Notes Series vary widely in their student body numbers, staff size, and number of volumes. Despite this variety, the most typical profile of the survey responses was from libraries with 1,000 to 2,500 students (49%), 10-20 staff (45%), and 100,000-350,000 volumes (71%).

In total, exactly seventy percent of the 214 responding libraries had conducted at least one survey on library use in the last five yearr. (If the number of libraries intending to survey in the near future are added, this figure increases to seventy-three percent.) This level of participation appears to be rather constant with the following qualifications: Libraries with over 5000 students tend to survey at a higher rate, yet when these libraries reach over 30 staff or over 800,000 volumes they tend to survey at a lower rate.

From the 131 libraries that indicated the number of surveys conducted, most libraries (70%) conducted either one or two user surveys in the past five years, with an additional portion (21%) conducting either three or four surveys. The remaining portion (9%) conducted from five to twenty surveys. One institution even reported that it had conducted forty surveys in the past five years.

Both non-surveying and surveying libraries responded to a large degree (60% and 74% respectively) that the most frequent reason not to conduct surveys was the lack of staff time. In addition, nearly two-thirds (65%) of the non-surveying institutions perceived lack of funding to be a restraint. In contrast, lack of funding was noted as a hindrance to conducting additional surveys for only fifteen percent of those institutions already conducting surveys.

Survey Type and Methodology (Questions 5-6)

Even though user satisfaction/dissatisfaction surveys were most prevalent (86%), nearly half of the respondents used surveys to make needs assessments (52%) and asked for user reactions to library products or services (46%).

Although the majority (90%) relied on the traditional written survey format, those who initiated alternative survey methods such as focus groups (14%) and interviews (14%) reported that a combination of both methods was more effective than employing just one method alone. The ability to interact with the survey participants:

- helped to overcome any deficiencies in the survey questions

- provided an opportunity for new questions to arise

- provided an opportunity to clarify areas of concern or misunderstanding among both the surveyors and those surveyed

Survey Motivation and Support (Questions 7-13)

One heartening result was that respondents indicated that surveys tended to be initiated more frequently by the library to improve programs and services (86%), rather than by an external mechanism such as accreditation (37%), program review (11%), or institutional administration's request (8%).

In correspondence to the preponderance of library-initiated surveys, exactly one-half (50%) of the surveying libraries relied on internal library resources alone to plan, fund, and implement the survey. In contrast, nearly one-half (48%) relied on the expertise of a faculty or staff member with survey research experience.

Individuals (either alone or with assistance) carried a slight majority of the load in the writing (52%), distribution (50%), and compilation (62%) of user surveys. Although the public services/instruction librarian was most frequently named as the person with the greatest survey responsibility, other library personnel were identified as participants also, including the head librarian, librarians, library staff, and student workers. Additional assistance was provided by external groups composed of administrators, faculty, and/or students. Although group sizes ranged from two to twenty, the ideal size suggested by several respondents was between five and eight members.

A majority indicated that the most useful printed source of information that they used in developing their survey came from the journal literature (33%) or books (20%) written for librarians. Another fifth of the respondents did not use any printed resources for assistance. The following two titles were frequently suggested as exceptionally useful (twenty-one and ten times respectively):

> Van House, Nancy, Beth T. Well, and Charles R. McClure. *Measuring Academic Library Performance: A Practical Approach.* Chicago: American Library Association, 1990.

> ALA Survey, *College and Research Libraries News* 55 (1994): 63.

Survey Use and Evaluation (Questions 14-18)

Most respondents indicated that their user survey provided useful or very useful information (84%) and were satisfied or very satisfied with the survey process used (86%), while a small minority expressed dissatisfaction with the usefulness of the survey responses (2%) or with the survey process used (6%). Yet, the need for survey composers to refer to other sources of expertise, such as this book, is demonstrated by the small number (16%) who were "very satisfied."

While nearly two-thirds of the respondents shared the results with their institutional administration (65%), library committee (65%), and library staff (63%), only one-third shared the results with their library users (33%). Several respondents noted that communication of the survey results back to the library users is an essential component of the survey process.

Survey results were most frequently used (52%) to make changes in services and staffing. The results were used to a lesser degree (36%) to make changes in policies and procedures. Few libraries (2%) indicated that surveys were incorporated into personnel evaluations. Even fewer (1%) did nothing with the results.

In the opening words of *Anna Karenina*, Tolstoi states that "Happy families are all alike; every unhappy family is unhappy in its own way." Much the same could be said about the diversity of problems in surveying. No single problem was shared by more than a third of the respondents. The two most noted problems were related to distribution--low response rate (29%) and reaching non-users (27%).

All of the other problems that registered over a ten-percent response related to insufficient planning and field-testing of the survey instrument. (A more complete elaboration of the problems appears under question 17 of the *Clip Notes* Survey Results section.) As responding libraries continually noted, planning is essential to survey success.

The most useful responses from those with survey experience were provided in the advice section. This advice is best summarized by the single word: "plan."

- Plan to have a clear purpose for your survey.
- Plan to promote and distribute the survey at a time when users will be most responsive
- Plan to pre-test your survey with others, especially non-librarians.
- Plan to use alternatives to the traditional written survey.
- Plan to accept and act on the results of the survey.

(A more complete elaboration of advice appears under question 18 of the *Clip Notes Survey Results* section.)

SELECTED BIBLIOGRAPHY

Association of Research Libraries. *User Surveys in ARL Libraries: A SPEC Kit*. SPEC Kit #205. Washington, D.C.: Association of Research Libraries, 1994.

Berger, Kenneth W. and Richard W. Hines. "What Does the User *Really* Want? The Library User Survey Project at Duke University." *The Journal of Academic Librarianship* 20 (1994): 306-309.

Bookstein, Abraham, and A. Lindsay, "Questionnaire Ambiguity: a Rasch Scaling Model Analysis." *Library Trends* 38 (1989): 215-236.

Breen, George Edward, and Albert Blankenship. *Do-It Yourself Marketing Research*. 3rd ed. New York: McGraw-Hill, 1989.

Busha, Charles H. and Stephen P. Harter. "Survey Research in Librarianship," in *Research Methods in Librarianship: Techniques and Interpretation*. New York: Academic Press, 1980, pp. 53-90.

Butler, Meredith, and Bonnie Gratch. "Planning a User Study - The Process Defined." *College and Research Libraries* 42 (1982): 320-330.

DeVellis, Robert F. *Scale Development: Theory and Application*. Newbury Park, CA: Sage Publications, 1991.

Fowler, Floyd, J. *Survey Research Methods*. Rev. ed. Newbury Park, CA: Sage Publications, 1988.

Glazier, Jack D., and Ronald R. Powell, eds. *Qualitative Research in Information Management*. Englewood, CO: Libraries Unlimited, 1992.

Gothberg, Helen M. "The Library Survey: a Research Methodology Rediscovered." *College and Research Libraries* 51 (1990): 553-559.

Hernon, Peter and Charles McClure. *Evaluation and Library Decision Making*. Norwood, NJ: Ablex, 1990.

Kidston, James S. "The Validity of Questionnaire Responses." *The Library Quarterly* 55 (1985): 133-150.

Lancaster, F. Wilfrid. *If You Want to Evaluate Your Library*. 2nd ed. Champaign, IL: University of Illinois, Graduate School of Library and Information Science, 1993.

Lavrakas, Paul J. *Telephone Survey Methods: Sampling, Selection, and Supervision*. 2nd ed. Newbury Park, CA: Sage Publications, 1993.

Morgan, David L., ed. *Succesful Focus Groups: Advancing the State of the Art*. Newbury Park, CA: Sage Publications, 1993.

Morris, Lynn Lyons, et al. *How to Measure Attitudes*. Vol. 6 of *Program Evaluation Kit*. 2nd ed. Beverly Hills, CA: Sage Publications, 1987.

Oppenheim, Abraham N. *Questionnaire Design, Interviews and Attitude Measurement*. New York: St. Martin's Press, 1992.

Payne, Stanley L. *The Art of Asking Questions*. Princeton, NJ: Princeton University Press, 1951.

Schlicter, Doris J. and J. Michael Pemberton. "The Emperor's New Clothes? Problems of the User Survey as a Planning Tool in Academic Libraries." *College and Research Libraries* 53 (1992): 257-265.

Schuman, Howard, and Stanley Presser. *Questions and Answers in Attitude Surveys: Experiments on Question Form, Wording, and Context*. New York: Academic Press, 1981.

Shaw, Marvin H. *Scales for the Measurement of Attitudes*. New York: McGraw-Hill, 1967.

Stewart, David W. and Prem N. Shamdasani. *Focus Groups: Theory and Practice*. Newbury Park, CA: Sage Publications, 1990.

Sudman, Seymour, and Norman M Bradburn. *Asking Questions: A Practical Guide to Question Design*. San Francisco: Jossey Bass, 1987.

Van House, Nancy A., Beth T. Weil, and Charles R. McClure. *Measuring Academic Library Performance: A Practical Approach*. Chicago: American Library Association, 1990.

Walker, Thomas D. "The First Use of a Library Questionnaire: Adalbert Blumenschein's Eighteenth-Century Study of European Libraries." *Library and Information Science Research* 16 (1994): 59-66.

Widdows, Richard, Tia A. Hensler, and Marlaya H. Wyncott, "The Focus Group Interview: A Method for Assessing Users' Evaluation of Library Service." *College and Research Libraries* 52 (1991): 352-359.

Zweizig, Douglas L. "Measuring Library Use." *Drexel Library Quarterly* 13 (1977): 3-15.

PLANNING GRID

PURPOSE	TO WHAT USE WILL THE INFORMATION BE PUT	QUESTION
To identify those college libraries which have conducted user surveys	Compilers will select sample surveys from this group	4
To determine if size of institution and library staff, correlates with the number of user surveys conducted	Those planning surveys will have a sense of what is possible with their staff	1, 2, 3
To identify a variety of user surveys that others have conducted.	By showing that a variety of surveys is possible, encourage librarians to consider doing user surveys	5, 6
To determine the variety of motivations that have led other librarians to develop user surveys	By showing the rdasons that other librarians have done surveys, encourage librarians to consider doing user surveys	7
To ascertain a variety of ways in which survey results have been used	By identifying a variety of ways that surveys are useful, encourage libraries to consider doing user surveys	15
To identify campus expertise and labor that librarians have used	To encourage librarians to seek out campus expertise and help	8, 13
To ascertain what parts of the surveys led to difficulties and what kind of problems occurred	Identifying specific problems that librarians should avoid in developing user surveys	17, 18, 19
To seek advice from librarians	To generate ideas, and also to allow for one open-ended question as recommended in survey research	18
To determine which librarians have not conducted surveys	To encourage librarians who have not done surveys to return the questionnaire	14
To identify printed resources which librarians used	Identify the most helpful resources for librarians doing surveys	12
To determine the number of staff involved in conducting surveys	To help other librarians determine staff load necessary	9, 10, 11

April 10, 1995

TO: College Library Directors Participating in CLIP Notes

FROM: Mignon Adams   Jeffrey Beck
            Philadelphia College of Pharmacy   University Libraries Mall
               and Science   Eastern Washington University
            4200 Woodland Avenue   Cheney, WA 99004
            Philadelphia, PA 19104-4491   jbeck@ewu.edu
            adams@hslc.org

RE: A Survey for *CLIP Notes*

Thank you for agreeing to help in the compilation of *CLIP Notes*, collections of documents gathered from college libraries and published by the College Libraries Section of the Association of College and Research Libraries.

We are currently working on a *CLIP Note* entitled *USER SURVEYS IN COLLEGE LIBRARIES*. Enclosed is a *CLIP Notes* survey which should take no more than 10 minutes to complete.

If you have administered user surveys in the last five years, we would very much like a copy of them. If you have **NOT** - we still want to hear from you (you'll need even less time to complete the survey).

Enclosed should be an addressed mailing label. If it is missing, please send the completed survey to Mignon Adams at the address listed above.

Your participation has been the reason for the success of *CLIP Notes*. Thank you very much for your help.

PLEASE RESPOND BY MAY 1.

CLIP NOTES SURVEY RESULTS

[N.B. Percentages do not total 100% due to rounding and multiple responses. Responses are reported in rank order, not in the order as they appeared in the original survey.]

A. Institution Profile

1. What is the approximate FTE student enrollment at your institution? (n=214)

up to 1000	12%
1000-2500	49%
2500-5000	27%
5000-7500	10%
over 7500	3%

2. How large is your staff (include both professional and support) (n=212)

up to nine FTE	24%
10-20	45%
20-30	18%
over 30	13%

3. How many volumes are in your library? (n=214)

up to 100,000	11%
100,000-350,000	71%
350,000-800,000	15%
over 800,000	3%

B. Survey Information: Background

4. Has your library conducted at least one survey that included questions about library use in the last five years?   Yes 70% (n=170)   No 30% (n=64) (total n=214)

If yes, how many?   (n=131)

one	40%
two	30%
three	11%
four	10%
five	5%
six	2%
nine	1%
twenty three	1%
forty	1%

5. What types of surveys have been conducted? (Check all that apply.) (n=150)

User satisfaction/dissatisfaction	86%
Needs assessment (to determine unmet service needs)	52%
User reactions to particular products or services	46%
Other.	11%
--library hours/environment/facilities	6%
--to assess library skills	1%
--student assistant employment assessment	1%
--identify users from other colleges	1%
--faculty survey	1%
--library stress	1%

6. What survey methods have been used? (Check all that apply.) (n=150)

Written Survey	90%
Focus groups (a group interview conducted by an outside facilitator)	14%
Individual interviews	7%
Group interviews	7%
Telephone surveys	5%
Other	3%
--online survey	1%
--e-mail survey	1%
--entrance into library survey	1%

7. Why were these surveys undertaken? (Check all that apply.) (n=150)

To improve programs/service	86%
To provide evidence of student attitudes or feelings	76%
To establish usage patterns	50%
To respond to student concerns	43%
For accreditation purposes	37%
To establish a case for new services	37%
To help staff make informed decisions about purchases	25%
For general feedback - no real purpose in mind	22%
To inform users about services	21%
As part of a mandated program review	11%
To plan for a new building	10%
Request from institutional administration	8%
To gather feedback from users to incorporate into personnel evaluation	8%
To determine services to be dropped	8%
Other.	16%

    --to determine what services are used by non-affiliated users
    --to modify staff behavior
    --to obtain feedback directly from users (instead of staff)
    --to assess user library skills
    --as part of research for dissertation by librarian
    --as part of college-wide assessment program
    --as part of marketing class
    --as part of strategic planning process initiated by the library
    --required by grant
    --needs assessment
    --evaluate mission effectiveness
    --preliminary preparation for focus group study

8. Check what additional resources (if any) that you made use of for your survey (n=150)

None	50%
A campus consultant	14%
Additional institutional funding	11%
Volunteers from outside the library	11%
Additional institutional staffing	8%
Grant funding	7%
An outside consultant	5%
Other	10%
--intern from library school	

9. The survey was written by (check one only) (n=154)
    One staff member with considerable input from others. 37%
    One staff member. 15%
    A group of staff members. How many? 28%
      (Ranged from 2 to 20.)
   Other. Who? 20%
      --faculty library committee
      --graduate student
      --campus learning taskforce
      --campus assessment committee with librarian representative
      --librarians from a regional consortium
      --based on another survey
      --a consultant

10. The survey was distributed by (check one only): (n=129)
    A group of staff members. 46%
    One staff member with some help from others. 28%
    One staff member. 22%
    Question does not apply, no printed survey used. 4%
    Other
      --by campus mail
      --by e-mail
      --placed at service point

11. Results of the survey were compiled by (Check one only) (n=157)
    One staff member. 40%
    One staff member with some help from others. 22%
    A group of staff members. 15%
    Campus office outside the library 14%
    Other 12%
      --Campus task force
      --Marketing class

12. Which of the following printed resources did you find **MOST** useful in developing your survey? (check
    only one): (n=167)
    Articles from library literature 33%
    Books written for librarians 20%
    Used no print resources 20%
    Literature from other disciplines
      (e.g., business, sociology) 9%
    SPEC kits from the Association of Research Libraries 9%
    Other 20%
      --input from faculty, staff, students, and other colleagues
      --previous surveys done by library
      --question to listserv

If you remember the title of a specific source that you found exceptionally useful, please list it:

  Van House, Nancy, Beth T. Well, and Charles R. McClure. *Measuring Academic Library Performance:
    A Practical Approach.* Chicago: American Library Association, 1990. (n=21)

  "ALA Survey." *College and Research Libraries News* (February 1994): 63. (n=10)

  "American Libraries Survey." *American Libraries* (March 1994): 279-280. (n=1)

C. Survey Information Use and Evaluation

13. Check any campus expertise (if any) you used for your surveys: (check all that apply) (n=150)

Faculty or staff member with survey research experience	48%
A campus unit to provide survey assistance	14%
Students enrolled in a course concerned with surveys	11%
Institutional computer center	11%
Other	3%

14. Did the results of the survey provide you with useful information? (n=147)

Useful	48%
Very useful	36%
Somewhat useful	14%
Not very useful	2%

15. What was done with the results? (Check all that apply.) (n=150)

Report written for institutional administration	65%
Results shared with library committee	65%
Comments circulated among library staff	63%
Report written for internal library use	58%
Changes made in services and/or staffing	52%
Changes made in policies and/or procedures	36%
Results communicated to library users	33%
Changes made in purchasing decisions	16%
Incorporated into personnel evaluation	2%
Nothing	1%
Other	14%

        --Presented at professional meeting
        --Incorporated into dissertation research
        --Shared with entire college community
        --Incorporated in accreditation report
        --Shared with regional library consortium
        --Full staff meeting to discuss results

16. How satisfied were you with the process you used? (n=143)

Satisfied	70%
Very satisfied	16%
Neither satisfied nor unsatisfied	8%
Unsatisfied	5%
Very dissatisfied	1%

17. Check all problems that occurred (n=150)

Low number of responses received	29%
Figuring out how to get the survey to both library users and non-users	27%
People responded to questions differently from what was expected	15%
After reviewing responses, realized that impnrtant questions were NOT asked	15%
After receiving responses, realized that some questions were not needed	13%
Survey results gave no new information	12%
Lack of support from college administration	7%
Low staff cooperation	4%

Other   15%

> --too much data to compile and to analyze
> --purpose of survey unclear--therefore some poorly worded and useless questions were asked
> --unscientific methodology
> --lack of shared goals
> --too many institutions involved, wanting too much information from one survey
> --unanticipated bias (e.g. "group think", peer influence, and limited student library experiences)
> --students who visit the library several times during the survey period get annoyed with the process
> --survey responses predictable
> --not enough time to evaluate results and incorporate into planning cycle
> --students not taking survey seriously (as evidenced by some of the responses)
> --low faculty responses

18. What advice would you give to another librarian planning a survey?

> "Take the results with a grain of salt. As in all aspects of life 'blowing one's horn' will only lead to negative results. The report [of survey results] should be full of subtle understatement."

> "Always remember that students and faculty are conditioned to like libraries and librarians.... Positives should be divided by 10 and negatives multiplied by 10."

> "Surveying is a very *imperfect* science. You will not get 'perfect' results. You need to have a somewhat relaxed attitude about the results and particularly any comments. Learn from patron suggestions but don't take things personally."

Advice fell into the following areas:

Timing/distribution
> --survey when students are less busy
> --include survey with packet for new students
> --review distribution procedure with staff and solicit suggestions in order to gain their
>   support and minimize workflow disruptions
> --provide incentive for users to complete survey
> --promote the survey and its results
> --survey regularly to measure changes over time
> --use anonymous drop box to collect responses

Planning
> --decide what information you want to survey
> --have a clear goal or purpose to obtain this information
> --plan early
> --plan for conducting additional surveys if response rate is low
> --pre-test the survey with novice users and survey experts
> --involve the whole staff or others outside of library
> --use focus groups or campus e-mail to develop the survey
> --consider how the data will be analyzed before writing the survey
> --comments may be difficult to compile
> --ask for support, including release time
> --don't create an "in-house, home-grown" survey
> --don't try to use one survey to evaluate every issue
> --think from the users' perspective
> --identify staff and statistical software package that will be used
> --maintain a list on-going concerns in case the administration requires you to conduct a survey
> --consider communicating the importance of the survey to users who do not want to be interrupted

Format

–use simple, short, focussed, structured surveys

–allow some open-ended responses, but do not use too many open-ended questions since the results are difficult to compile and some comments may not answer the intended question

–provide "not applicable" or "no opinion" options

–include a variety of instruments and methods beyond the written survey, such as a telephone exit interview of graduating students or an open-ended e-mail survey

–for focus groups, use a competent facilitator, communicate with participants after the focus group, implement some of the ideas and suggestions immediately, a focus group comprised of users and non-users may be better than a survey of users alone

–avoid using library jargon

–try to frame the questions positively (e.g. students should be made to feel part of the solution to a "behavior" problem in the library and not just the cause of the problem itself)

–only ask questions that give answers could change how you do (or plan to do) something

–only ask demographic questions that potentially divide responses

Results

–act on the results

–use a Scantron form

–acknowledge that the results may be inconclusive

–allow time to compile results

–expect to be surprised by the results

–don't expect specific answers

–be willing to accept what users suggest

–surveys are timeconsuming and worthless if not used

D. Survey Information: Non-participation

19. What reasons have prevented your institution from conducting any surveys **OR** additional surveys? (Check all that apply.)

No surveys conducted due to (n=64)

Lack of staff time	74%
Lack of funding	65%
Most issues are pretty well understood-survey not necessary	29%
Lack of expertise (in formulating and conducting survey)	24%
Skeptical about the benefits of surveys	20%
Never found anything we needed to survey	10%
Other included:	35%
–planning on surveying soon	11%
–low priority	8%
–too many other things to do	5%
–suggestion box in use	5%
–user fatigue in answering surveys	5%
–do not want to overdo surveys	5%

Additional surveys not conducted due to (n=150)

Lack of staff time	60%
Most issues are pretty well understood-survey not necessary	19%
Lack of funding	15%
Lack of expertise (in formulating and conducting survey)	15%
Skeptical about the benefits of surveys	13%
Never found anything we needed to survey	5%

General Surveys

Eckerd College
A brief, easily administered and machine-scored measure of user satisfaction.

Goucher College
Adapts a semantic differential scale to measure overall satisfaction.

Bradley University
In addition to measuring faculty satisfaction and frequency of use, includes a way to identify those who want more information.

Trinity College of Vermont
An elegant and simple way to provide a "snapshot" of user satisfaction.

Williams College
In-depth survey of faculty feelings towards collection and relationship to library.

STUDENT LIBRARY SURVEY, 1993-1994

The purpose of this survey is to solicit your feedback regarding the support of the library for your education at Eckerd College. Many of the statements are drawn from the "Mission of Eckerd College" and the "Statement of Purposes of the Eckerd College Library." This survey is important in helping to determine the resources, services, and assistance you need. Please help us help you. Use a #2 pencil. Do not fold survey.

Major:_____ Collegium ☐ BES ☐ CCU ☐ CRA ☐ FDN ☐ LET ☐ NAS

Class ☐ FR ☐ SO ☐ JR ☐ SR
Do you live off-campus? ☐ Yes ☐ No
Are you a transfer student? ☐ Yes ☐ No

How well does the library provide the following. . .

1=Very Poorly 2=Poorly 3=Well 4=Very Well

circulation periods that allow sufficient time for use   ☐1 ☐2 ☐3 ☐4
appropriate study environment   ☐1 ☐2 ☐3 ☐4
books in your major   ☐1 ☐2 ☐3 ☐4
journals in your major   ☐1 ☐2 ☐3 ☐4
open hours to encourage use of its collections   ☐1 ☐2 ☐3 ☐4

How well does the library support the following goals of Eckerd College. . .

breadth of learning   ☐1 ☐2 ☐3 ☐4
ability to perform in-depth research   ☐1 ☐2 ☐3 ☐4
learning how to be an independent user of the library   ☐1 ☐2 ☐3 ☐4
examining materials to encounter and evaluate alternative viewpoints   ☐1 ☐2 ☐3 ☐4
understanding how recorded knowledge is organized and structured within the library   ☐1 ☐2 ☐3 ☐4

During the past semester, how often did you use the Eckerd College Library?

☐ almost every day
☐ a few times each week
☐ a few times each month
☐ a few times each semester
☐ almost never

For the following questions: 1 = 75% or more 2 = 50 to 74% 3 = 25 to 49% 4 = 24% or less 5 = Did not use library

During the past semester, what percent of the books that you needed did you locate in the library?   ☐1 ☐2 ☐3 ☐4 ☐5

During the past semester, what percent of the journals and magazines that you needed did you locate in the library?   ☐1 ☐2 ☐3 ☐4 ☐5

Approximately for what percent of your courses taken within the past year have you had to use other area libraries to complete your library-related assignments?   ☐1 ☐2 ☐3 ☐4 ☐5

How many books and journal articles have you borrowed within the past year from other libraries through interlibrary loan?   ☐0 ☐1-2 ☐3-5 ☐>5

How many courses have you taken during your academic career at Eckerd College that require substantial library related assignments (seminar papers, research papers, literature reviews)?   ☐0 ☐1-2 ☐3-5 ☐>5

How many courses, including Autumn and Winter Term, have you taken at Eckerd College in which you have received instructions from a librarian in class on how to use the library?   ☐0 ☐1 ☐2 ☐3 ☐>3

What time of day do you most frequently make use of the library? (Please check all that apply)

Mornings ☐
Afternoons ☐
Early Evenings ☐
Late Evenings ☐
Saturday afternoons ☐
Sunday Afternoons ☐

What other times would you most want the library to be open? (Please check all that apply)

Friday evenings ☐
Earlier Saturday Mornings ☐
Saturday Evenings ☐
Sunday Mornings ☐
Later on Weekday Evenings ☐
Earlier on Weekday Mornings ☐
Current Hours Are Adequate ☐
Other ☐

PLEASE MAKE COMMENTS OR SUGGESTIONS ON THE BACK OF THIS SHEET

BPM form #04-14-1994 11:41 Generated by Scanning Dynamics Inc software.

ADAPTED FROM A SURVEY CREATED BY DIANA CUNNINGHAM, NEW YORK MEDICAL COLLEGE AND ROB PERNICK, PRIVATE CONSULTANT

GUIDELINES FOR COMPLETING THE SURVEY

This survey is anonymous, fairly brief yet essential to our library's ability to provide quality service to you, our customer. There are no right or wrong answers, nor are there any "trick" questions.

The survey contains multiple choice, word pair questions and a few open-ended questions. For each multiple choice question circle the word or phrase that comes closest to your view. Some questions may be difficult to answer because you do not have enough knowledge, experience or opinions about the topic. In these cases circle the "NOT SURE" option.

PART I - SATISFACTION WITH LIBRARY SERVICES

A. REFERENCE SERVICES- these services include answering questions of all types and complexity, providing orientations to the library, delivering training and conducting computer searches.

Generally speaking, to what extent are reference services (circle your answer):

1.	Helpful.....	Very Little	Little	Some	Great	Very Great	Not Sure
2.	Timely......	Very Little	Little	Some	Great	Very Great	Not Sure
3.	Friendly....	Very Little	Little	Some	Great	Very Great	Not Sure
4.	Convenient...	Very Little	Little	Some	Great	Very Great	Not Sure

B. INTERLIBRARY LOAN SERVICES - this service obtains books or photocopies of journal articles from other libraries.

Generally speaking, to what extent is the Interlibrary Loan service (circle your answer):

5.	Helpful.....	Very Little	Little	Some	Great	Very Great	Not Sure
6.	Timely......	Very Little	Little	Some	Great	Very Great	Not Sure
7.	Friendly....	Very Little	Little	Some	Great	Very Great	Not Sure
8.	Convenient...	Very Little	Little	Some	Great	Very Great	Not Sure

C.   SERVICES OF THE CIRCULATION DEPARTMENT - these services include circulating materials into and out of the library, processing faculty reserves of materials needed for course reserve and searching for missing items.

Generally speaking, to what extent are the services of the Circulation department (circle your answer):

9.	Helpful.....	Very Little	Little	Some	Great	Very Great	Not Sure
10.	Timely......	Very Little	Little	Some	Great	Very Great	Not Sure
11.	Friendly....	Very Little	Little	Some	Great	Very Great	Not Sure
12.	Convenient...	Very Little	Little	Some	Great	Very Great	Not Sure

PART II - SATISFACTION WITH INFORMATION RESOURCES

As an academic library we have various books, journals, reference manuals, etc. and non-print materials such as videotapes and recordings to assist you in your studies.

Generally speaking, to what extent are you satisfied with the following information resources (circle your answer):

13.	Books.....	Very Little	Little	Some	Great	Very Great	Not Sure
14.	Periodicals..	Very Little	Little	Some	Great	Very Great	Not Sure
15.	Videos......	Very Little	Little	Some	Great	Very Great	Not Sure
16.	CD-ROM Databases.... (ex. PsycLIT Academic Index, Humanities Index, Social Sciences Index etc.)	Very Little	Little	Some	Great	Very Great	Not Sure
17.	Microfilm ...	Very Little	Little	Some	Great	Very Great	Not Sure

18.	Recordings.	Very Little	Little	Some	Great	Very Great	Not Sure

What else should we know about the library's Information Resources? Stated differently, are we providing you the best environment in which to learn? How can we improve?

PART III - SATISFACTION WITH PHYSICAL RESOURCES

Satisfaction with physical resources can mean a number of things such as: comfort, ease of usage, convenient location, availability, etc.

Generally speaking, to what extent are you satisfied with the library's (circle your answer):

19.	Group study rooms	Very Little	Little	Some	Great	Very Great	Not Sure
20.	Individual study carrels................	Very Little	Little	Some	Great	Very Great	Not Sure
21.	Heating, cooling and ventilation...........	Very Little	Little	Some	Great	Very Great	Not Sure
22.	Lighting	Very Little	Little	Some	Great	Very Great	Not Sure
23.	Copy machines............	Very Little	Little	Some	Great	Very Great	Not Sure
24.	Public telephones.............	Very Little	Little	Some	Great	Very Great	Not Sure
25.	Quietness................	Very Little	Little	Some	Great	Very Great	Not Sure

26.	Furniture..........	Very Little	Little	Some	Great	Very Great	Not Sure
27.	Cleanliness.........	Very Little	Little	Some	Great	Very Great	Not Sure
28.	Security: personal and property	Very Little	Little	Some	Great	Very Great	Not Sure
29.	Physical accessibility...........	Very Little	Little	Some	Great	Very Great	Not Sure

Other aspects of the library's physical resources that influence your experience include:

PART IV - GENERAL REACTIONS

We ask you for a more subjective reaction in this final section. Each pair of words could describe the library. For instance, in the first questions if you feel that, on balance, the library is responsive to your needs check the box closest to the word "responsive." If you feel that the library is generally speaking, nonresponsive to your concerns check the box closest to the word "indifferent." If you experience the library as a mix of responsiveness and indifference, check the box in the middle of the line. Use this same method for all nine questions.

For each pair, check the box which you believe best describes your experiences in the library.

30.	Responsive	[ ]	[ ]	[ ]	[ ]	[ ]	Indifferent
31.	Disorganized	[ ]	[ ]	[ ]	[ ]	[ ]	Organized
32.	Experienced	[ ]	[ ]	[ ]	[ ]	[ ]	Inexperienced
33.	Hostile	[ ]	[ ]	[ ]	[ ]	[ ]	Friendly
34.	Excellent	[ ]	[ ]	[ ]	[ ]	[ ]	Inferior

35.	Status Quo	[ ]	[ ]	[ ]	[ ]	[ ]	Progressive
36.	Inviting	[ ]	[ ]	[ ]	[ ]	[ ]	Unpleasant
37.	Traditional	[ ]	[ ]	[ ]	[ ]	[ ]	Innovative
38.	Fast	[ ]	[ ]	[ ]	[ ]	[ ]	Slow

TWO FINAL QUESTIONS:

What in the library needs immediate attention?

What should we know about our services, information resources, physical environment or anything else?

FACTUAL INFORMATION SHEET

You will remain anonymous in this survey. The questions asked here will allow data analysis by categories, for example, organizational unit. No data will be reported by individuals.

Gender   (Circle your answer)

       Female
       Male

Race   (Circle number of your answer)

1. African American
2. Asian/Oriental
3. Hispanic
4. Native American
5. White American
6. Other

On average, how many times a week do you use the library?   (Circle your response)

0   1-2   3-4   5-6   7 or more

What is your academic major?

_____

Length of time at Goucher College (round to nearest year) _____

Thank you very much for making the Julia Rogers Library more responsive to your needs.

(to mail fold on dotted line)

Margie Simon

Library

Campus Mail

Faculty Perception of Library Services

Please help us improve Library Service by answering these questions.
Please circle the appropriate answers.

Library Services	Rate your level of satisfaction			How often do you use this service?				Check here to receive more info.
	Not Satisfied	Somewhat Satisfied	Satisfied	Never	Less than once per month	About once per month	More than once per month	
1. Online Catalog	1	2	3	a	b	c	d	☐
2. IBIS	1	2	3	a	b	c	d	☐
3. CARL	1	2	3	a	b	c	d	☐
4. CD-ROM Indexes	1	2	3	a	b	c	d	☐
5. Document Delivery	1	2	3	a	b	c	d	☐
6. Interlibrary Loan	1	2	3	a	b	c	d	☐
7. Online Search Services (conducted by librarians)	1	2	3	a	b	c	d	☐
8. Liaison Librarian	1	2	3	a	b	c	d	☐
9. Librarian-provided library instruction for your classes	1	2	3	a	b	c	d	☐
10. Reference Desk Service	1	2	3	a	b	c	d	☐
11. Library portions of BUINFO and WWW	1	2	3	a	b	c	d	☐
12. Acquisitions (ordering materials)	1	2	3	a	b	c	d	☐
13. Approval books	1	2	3	a	b	c	d	☐
14. FirstSearch Services	1	2	3	a	b	c	d	☐
15. OCLC	1	2	3	a	b	c	d	☐
16. Reserves	1	2	3	a	b	c	d	☐
17. Music Resource Center	1	2	3	a	b	c	d	☐
18. Special Collections	1	2	3	a	b	c	d	☐

Please use the back of this form, or attach an additional sheet,
if you have any comments. We would appreciate specific comments on
improving current services, and/or ideas for new services at Bradley.

Department _____   Full-time ☐   Part-time ☐

Instructor ☐   Asst. Prof. ☐   Assoc. Prof. ☐   Prof. ☐

Name (optional, please include if requesting additional info.) _____

Please return to E. Hansen in the Library.

Thank you for using the Trinity Library. To better serve you, we are conducting a survey. Please take a moment to answer these questions about your visit here today:

Please circle one:

Did you find information on the subject you were researching?   Yes   Some   No

Comments:

If you were looking for a specific item, did you find it?   Yes   No

Comments:

How would you evaluate the helpfulness and responsiveness of the staff?   Excellent   Good   Poor

Comments:

Please deposit this in the survey box at the circulation desk. Thank you! Your input will help us improve our library service to you.

TRINITY COLLEGE
OF VERMONT

respondent's department   rank   name (optional)

ADEQUACY OF COLLEGE LIBRARY COLLECTIONS AND SERVICES

The Library Committee seeks the opinions of all faculty regarding the collections and services of the College Library. The questionnaire below is designed to identify areas in need of further development and to determine the priorities that best meet the needs of the Williams community.

We request that you take the few minutes necessary to answer the questions below, and return the questionnaire to David Booth in Hopkins Hall no later than <u>Monday, November 14.</u> Do not underestimate the importance of your response. The opinions that we receive will significantly influence the report of the Committee, which will be submitted to the Provost later this fall.

Feel free to contact any member of the Committee with questions or comments concerning this questionnaire or any other matter pertaining to this review. The members of the Committee are Larry Raab, Chair; Duane Bailey; David Booth; Jim Cubit; Phyllis Cutler; Georges Dreyfus; Mani Srinivasan '97, Robert Volz, and Christopher Warren '97.

A. COLLECTIONS

Indicate the adequacy of each of the items listed below by marking the appropriate number next to it.

     1 - very good
     2 - adequate
     3 - not adequate
     4 - have not used

	(a) for your students	(b) for your research	(c) for enrichment
1. Books	_____	_____	_____
2. Periodicals	_____	_____	_____
3. CD-ROMs	_____	_____	_____
4. Government documents	_____	_____	_____
5. Videos	_____	_____	_____
6. Sound recordings	_____	_____	_____

2

7. Do you understand why the Library maintains a cap on the periodical budget? Circle <u>yes</u> or <u>no</u>. Comment if you wish.

8. Do you know about the university press program, whereby the Library automatically receives the publications of selected presses that fall within a subject profile? Circle <u>yes</u> or <u>no</u>. If yes, please comment on it.

9. Do you rely on other academic libraries for support of your work? Circle <u>yes</u> or <u>no</u>. If you rely on particular libraries, please name them.

10. If you rely on other academic libraries, how do you make use of them? Circle the letters that apply.

      a. through the library gateway to online catalogs
      b. through site visits

11. Are there any special needs that should be filled or important new directions taken in developing collections? Circle yes or no. Please specify.

B. SERVICES

    How satisfied are you with the services provided by the library? Mark the appropriate number next to each of the items that follow.

               1 - very satisfied
               2 - satisfied
               3 - not satisfied
               4 - have not used
               5 - unaware of

1. The online catalog (FRANCIS)   _____

2. Library classroom instruction   _____

3. Success rate for purchasing books that you request _____

4. Turnaround time from when books
are ordered to when they are received _____

5. Information services at the Reference Desk   _____

6. E-mail reference service   _____

7. Online search services   _____

8. The library gateway   _____

9. Interlibrary loan services

    a. Procurement of books   _____

    b. Document delivery   _____

    c. Rush document delivery using UnCover   _____

10. Circulation policies   _____

11. Reserve policies   _____

12. Library hours   _____

13. Off-hour library access   _____

14. Have you been assisted by a library liaison in ordering books? Circle yes or no. If yes, comment on the value to your department of having a contact person on the library staff with whom to work.

15. Are you satisfied that your requests for materials are given fair consideration by the faculty library coordinator of your department? Circle <u>yes</u> or <u>no</u>.

16. How long after orders for books have been placed would you expect to receive them?

    a. From domestic publishers   _____

    b. From foreign publishers   _____

    c. Out-of-print materials   _____

17. If the library has provided your classes with bibliographic instruction, has this resulted in an improvement in student papers? Circle <u>yes</u> or <u>no</u>. Please comment.

18. Have you attended a library workshop to introduce you to new electronic sources. Circle <u>yes</u> or <u>no</u>. Please comment on the value of this.

C. FACILITIES AND EQUIPMENT

Which campus libraries do you use? Circle the numbers of all that apply.

1 Sawyer
2 Biology
3 Chemistry
4 Physics/Astronomy
5 Math/Computer Science
6 Psychology
7 Center for Environmental Studies
8 Geology
9 Chapin
10 Archives

Indicate the adequacy of each of the items listed below by marking the appropriate number next to each of the items listed.

1 - very good
2 - adequate
3 - not adequate
4 - don't know

		(a) quantity	(b) quality
11.	Computer terminals	_____	_____
12.	Microfilm/fiche readers/printers	_____	_____
13.	Photocopy equipment	_____	_____
14.	Video viewing equipment	_____	_____
15.	Audio equipment	_____	_____
16.	Study spaces	_____	_____
17.	Lighting	_____	_____

Surveys Adapted from Other Surveys

American Library Association
A survey published in both *American Libraries* (March, 1994, p. 279), and *College and Research Library News* (February, 1994, p. 63) for libraries to distribute.

Our Lady of the Lake University
An example of an adaptation of the ALA survey.

Measuring Academic Library Performance (ALA, 1990)
A manual for the use of output measures which includes sample instruments. (See p. 99 for an example of a report analyzing the results of administering one of the surveys.)

Arkansas Tech University
Transylvania University
Examples of adapting instruments from *Measuring Academic Library Performance*.

How to do it

The customer satisfaction survey designed by ALA is intended as a tool to be used by all types of libraries, one that will generate direct feedback from those we value most — our customers.

Some tips for administering your customer service survey:

1. You may customize the survey by adding your library's name and logo in the space provided or by adding other questions that are pertinent to your library. Public libraries should "white out" the reference to students and faculty in Question 8. School and academic libraries should take out the reference to age.

2. Decide who will distribute the survey form. You may wish to recruit students or other volunteers for this task.

3. Decide when to distribute the form. We suggest that you distribute it for at least 12 hours during National Library Week, April 17-23, 1994.

4. Decide where to distribute the survey forms and who should get them. You may wish to station someone at the library main entrance or — at a grocery store. You may also hand out at speaking engagements. Or, send to all faculty members.

5. If necessary, you may leave survey forms and pencils on a desk with a sign inviting library users to respond. This should be in a supervised area.

6. Send a press release to local/campus media to make people aware that you are conducting a customer satisfaction survey. You may also want to send a follow-up release — "Library users give high marks for service" or "80 percent of library users say they want more hours."

7. Hold an orientation session for your survey team. Team members should be instructed to be encouraging — "We will really appreciate this" — but not overly persistent if someone clearly does not wish to participate. Have plenty of pencils to give out.

8. Make your survey visible. Post signs saying, "We want to hear from you. Please fill out a Customer Satisfaction Survey today." Have a large box clearly identified ("Return surveys here. Thank you.") to collect surveys.

9. Have a "coding party" with your survey team tabulating the results.

10. Record the total number of responses to each question and send the results by **May 15, 1994**, to: Customer Satisfaction Survey, ALA Public Information Office, 50 E. Huron St., Chicago, IL 60611. (Note: *Comments are primarily for your use. Send only those that you feel are particularly insightful or might be useful for ALA's legislative/publicity efforts.*) ●

Reprinted with permission from the American Library Association

---

(Add your library's logo or reproduce on library letterhead)

Customer Satisfaction Survey

Let us know what you think.

Our library staff wants to meet your needs. Please take a moment to answer these questions and let us know how we are doing. Place a check mark by the answer that applies.

1. How satisfied are you with our books and other services?
☐ Extremely ☐ Very ☐ Satisfied ☐ Somewhat ☐ Not at all

2. How helpful is our staff?
☐ Extremely ☐ Very ☐ Helpful ☐ Somewhat ☐ Not at all

3. How easy is it to find what you need?
☐ Extremely ☐ Very ☐ Easy ☐ Somewhat ☐ Not at all

4. How important is the library to you?
☐ Extremely ☐ Very ☐ Important ☐ Somewhat ☐ Not at all

5. How often do you visit the library or call for information?
☐ Weekly ☐ Monthly ☐ Four times a year ☐ Twice a year ☐ Once a year

6. How often do you ask a librarian for help?
☐ Weekly ☐ Monthly ☐ Four times a year ☐ Twice a year ☐ Once a year

7. Are there other things you would like the library to offer?
☐ More books ☐ More hours ☐ More reference materials
☐ Other *(please explain below)*

8. Are you? ☐ Under 18 ☐ 18 or older ☐ A student ☐ Faculty/staff ☐ Other

Please share your comments or suggestions about how we can improve our services to you.

_____

_____

_____

_____

Your name and telephone *(optional)*

_____

_____

This survey is being conducted in cooperation with the American Library Association and other libraries across the country for a national "snapshot" of library customer satisfaction. Thank you for taking time to comment.

Our Lady of the Lake University Libraries
Student Satisfaction Survey

LET US KNOW WHAT YOU THINK.

Our library staff wants to meet your information needs. Please take a moment to answer these questions and let us know how we are doing. Please darken the appropiate circle on the scantron sheet (using a number #2 pencil) and return both the scantron sheet and survey form to your instructor.

1. **How satisfied are you with our books?**
   a.____Extremely b.____Very c.____Satisfied d.____Somewhat e.____Not at all

2. **How satisfied are you with our journal holdings?**
   a.____Extremely b.____Very c.____Satisfied d.____Somewhat e.____Not at all

3. **How satisfied are you with our services?**
   a.____Extremely b.____Very c.____Satisfied d.____Somewhat e.____Not at all

4. **How helpful is our circulation staff?**
   a.____Extremely b.____Very c.____Helpful d.____Somewhat e.____Not at all

5. **How helpful are the reference librarians?**
   a.____Extremely b.____Very c.____Helpful d.____Somewhat e.____Not at all

6. **How easy is it to find what you need?**
   a.____Extremely b.____Very c.____Easy d.____Somewhat e.____Not at all

7. **How important is the library to you?**
   a.____Extremely b.____Very c.____Important d.____Somewhat e.____Not at all

8. **How often do you visit the library or call for information?**
   a.____Weekly b.____Twice a month c.____Monthly d.____Once a semester
   e.____Never

9. **How often do you ask a librarian for help?**
   a.____Weekly b.____Twice a month c.____Monthly d.____Once a semester
   e.____Never

10. **Are there other things you would like the library to offer?**
    a.____More books d.____More reference materials
    b.____More journals e.____More CD-ROM databases
    c.____More hours (Please use #12 for additional comments or suggestions.)

11. **Are you?**
    a.____A freshmen b.____A sophomore c.____A Junior d.____A senior
    e.____A graduate student

12. **Please share your comments or suggestions about how we can improve our services to you on the back of this sheet.**

Thank you for taking time to comment.

Form 1-1
General Satisfaction Survey

PLEASE HELP US IMPROVE LIBRARY SERVICE BY
ANSWERING A FEW QUESTIONS.

1. What did you do in the library today? For each, circle the number that best reflects how successful you were.

	Successful?					
	Did not do today	Not at all				Completely
Looked for books or periodicals	0	1	2	3	4	5
Studied	0	1	2	3	4	5
Reviewed current literature	0	1	2	3	4	5
Did a literature search (manual or computer)	0	1	2	3	4	5
Asked a reference question	0	1	2	3	4	5
Browsed	0	1	2	3	4	5
Returned books	0	1	2	3	4	5
Other (what?)_____	0	1	2	3	4	5

2. How easy was the library to use today? *(Circle one)*:

                       1   2   3   4   5

          Not at all easy   **Very easy**

        Why? _____

3. Overall, how satisfied are you with today's library visit? *(Circle one)*:

                       1   2   3   4   5

          Not at all satisfied   **Very satisfied**

        Why? _____

4. Today's visit was primarily in support of *(Check one)*:
    ___1. Course work   ___3. Teaching   ___5. A mix of several purposes
    ___2. Research   ___4. Current awareness ___6. Other:_____

5. You are *(Check one)*:
    ___1. Undergraduate   ___3. Faculty   ___5. Other staff
    ___2. Graduate student ___4. Research staff   ___6. Other (what?)_____

6. Your field *(Check one)*:
    ___1. Humanities ___2. Sciences ___3. Social Sciences ___4. Other (What?)_____

OTHER COMMENTS? Please use back of form.

Form 14-1
Reference Satisfaction Survey

PLEASE LET US KNOW HOW WE ARE DOING. Evaluate the *reference* service that you received today by circling one number on each of the following scales. Feel free to explain—use the back of the form.

If you were NOT asking a reference question today, please check here _____ and stop. Thank you.

1. *Relevance* of information provided:

    Not relevant   1   2   3   4   5   Very relevant

2. Satisfaction with the *amount* of information provided:

    Not satisfied   1   2   3   4   5   Very satisfied
    (too little, too much)   (the right amount)

3. *Completeness* of the answer that you received:

    Not complete   1   2   3   4   5   Very complete

4. *Helpfulness* of staff:

    Not helpful   1   2   3   4   5   Extraordinarily helpful

5. Overall, how *satisfied* are you?

    Not satisfied   1   2   3   4   5   Extremely satisfied

Why? _____

_____

6. You are:

    _____ 1. Undergraduate   _____ 4. Research staff
    _____ 2. Graduate student   _____ 5. Other staff
    _____ 3. Faculty   _____ 6. Other? _____

7. What will you use this information for?

    _____ 1. Course work   _____ 4. Mix of several purposes
    _____ 2. Research   _____ 5. Current awareness
    _____ 3. Teaching   _____ 6. Other? _____

THANK YOU! Please leave this questionnaire in the box.

USE BACK OF PAGE FOR ANY ADDITIONAL COMMENTS.

Arkansas Tech University

PLEASE HELP US IMPROVE LIBRARY SERVICE BY ANSWERING A FEW QUESTIONS

1. What did you do in the library <u>today</u>? For each, circle the number that best reflects how successful you were.

	Not Done Today	Not Successful	Moderately Successful	Completely Successful
Looked for books or periodicals	0	1	2	3
Studied	0	1	2	3
Reviewed current literature	0	1	2	3
Used an index for a literature search (either print or computer)	0	1	2	3
Asked reference question(s)	0	1	2	3
Browsed	0	1	2	3
Other (list & rate) _____		1	2	3
_____		1	2	3
_____		1	2	3

2. How <u>easy</u> was the library to use <u>today</u>? (circle one): **Not at all easy**   **Moderately**   **Very easy**
                                                                  1   2   3

   Why? _____

3. Overall, how <u>satisfied</u> are you with <u>today's</u> library visit? (circle one):

                                              Not at all satisfied   **Moderately**   **Very satisfied**
                                                    1   2   3

   Why? _____

4. Today's visit was primarily for (check one):
   __1. Class Assignment   __2. Teaching   __3. A mix of several purposes
   __4. Current Awareness   __5. Research   __6. Other:_____

3. You are (check one): __1. Freshman   __2. Sophomore __3. Junior   __4. Senior
                                __5. Grad Student __6. Faculty   __7. Staff   __8. Other(what?)_____

6. Your field (check one): __1. College of Arts & Sciences __2. Sch. of Business __3. Sch. of Education
                                __4. College of Bible & Rel.   __5. Sch. of Nursing   __6. Undecided

OTHER COMMENTS OR PREVIOUS EXPERIENCES? Please use back of form. Detailed, specific comments will be the most helpful for planning service improvements. Thank you for helping.

**PLEASE RETURN THIS SURVEY TO SURVEYOR OR FOLD IT AND DEPOSIT IT
IN THE QUESTIONNAIRE BOX NEAR THE EXIT GATE.**

TRANSYLVANIA UNIVERSITY LIBRARY
General Satisfaction Survey

PLEASE HELP US IMPROVE LIBRARY SERVICE BY
ANSWERING A FEW QUESTIONS.

1. What did you do in the library today? For each, circle the number that best reflects how successful you were.

		Successful?				
	Did not do today	Not at all				Completely
Looked for:	0	1	2	3	4	5
books	0	1	2	3	4	5
periodicals	0	1	2	3	4	5
Studied	0	1	2	3	4	5
Searched indexes (printed or computer)	0	1	2	3	4	5
Asked a reference question	0	1	2	3	4	5
Browsed	0	1	2	3	4	5
Returned books	0	1	2	3	4	5
Other (what?)	0	1	2	3	4	5

2. How <u>easy</u> was the library to use <u>today</u>? (<u>Circle one</u>):

    1   2   3   4   5

    Not at all easy   **Very easy**

    Why? _____

3. Overall, how <u>satisfied</u> are you with <u>today's</u> library visit? (<u>Circle one</u>):

    1   2   3   4   5

    Not at all satisfied   **Very satisfied**

    Why? _____

4. Today's visit was primarily in support of (<u>Check one</u>):
    ___1. Course work   ___3. Teaching   ___5. A mix of several purposes
    ___2. Research   ___4. Current awareness ___6. Other:_____

5. You are (<u>Check one</u>):
    ___1. TU student   ___3. TU staff   ___5. Other (What?)
    ___2. TU faculty   ___4. Community   _____
    If you came on behalf of a faculty member please check here _____

6. **FACULTY ONLY**
    Your division (<u>Check one</u>)
    1. Ed. & PE _____   3. Business _____   5. Natural Sci. _____
    2. Fine Arts _____   4. Humanities _____   6. Social Sci. _____

        Please indicate your program _____

OTHER COMMENTS? Please use back of form.

TRANSYLVANIA UNIVERSITY LIBRARY

Reference Satisfaction Survey

PLEASE LET US KNOW HOW WE ARE DOING. Evaluate the reference service that you received today by circling one number on each of the following scales. Feel free to explain on back of the form.

1. Relevance of information provided:

   Not relevant   1   2   3   4   5   Very relevant

2. Satisfaction with the amount of information provided:

   Not satisfied   1   2   3   4   5   Very satisfied
   (too little, too much)   (the right amount)

3. Completeness of the answer that you received:

   Not complete   1   2   3   4   5   Very complete

4. Helpfulness of staff:

   Not helpful 1   2   3   4   5   Extraordinarily helpful

5. Overall, how satisfied are you?

   Not satisfied   1   2   3   4   5   Extremely satisfied

Why?

_____

_____

6. You are:

   _____1. Student   _____3. Other staff

   _____2. Faculty   _____4. Other?_____

7. What will you use this information for?

   _____1. Course work   _____4. Mix of several purposes

   _____2. Research   _____5. Current awareness

   _____3. Teaching   _____6. Other?_____

THANK YOU! Please leave this questionnaire in the box.

USE BACK OF PAGE FOR ANY ADDITIONAL COMMENTS.

Surveys of Online Services

Drew University
A survey mounted on an online catalog to measure satisfaction with the catalog.

Walla Walla College
A very focused survey on a new computer menu.

State University of New York at Plattsburgh
A questionnaire asking for user reaction to a test of the online product, FIRSTSEARCH.

This online survey and corresponding transaction logs provided the primary data for a dissertation project. A questionnaire was administered online to all users of the system on twenty randomly-selected days during the academic semester. Students, staff and faculty used the online catalog either on the campus network with personal computers, in their offices and residence hall rooms, or terminals located in the library.

The questionnaire asked for limited demographic data and was designed to elicit information pertaining to hypotheses in a dissertation study. See Snelson (1993, 1994) to read about the findings of this study. The length of the questionnaire was short to encourage a high response rate. An introductory screen stated that the survey contained seventeen questions.

On the sample day, all transactions on the library system were logged so that information on browsing behavior and search strategy could be linked to the questionnaire data on accessibility and satisfaction.

Each time someone approached a terminal in the library or selected the online catalog option from the campus network on survey days, the initial screen briefly explained the project and asked for participation. If an individual declined to participate in the study, an open-ended question asked about the reason for not answering the survey. For those individuals who agreed to participate, the questionnaire appeared on their screen when they exited from the online catalog after finishing their search. Questions were displayed one at a time; respondents entered a number to answer questions using a Likert scale. There was a third option for repeat patrons who had already participated in the study. The response rate was 32 percent.

Users deciding not to complete a survey were asked to answer a single, open-ended question: Why did you not wish to participate in this study? Answers were reviewed and categorized.

Two sets of qualitative data were collected. The first contains open-ended responses to the final question of the online survey. Forty-five surveys or 22.3% of all respondents volunteered additional information. The second set of qualitative data consists of thirty interviews with users who had used the system from a remote location. The subjects were phoned and asked a series of questions about their remote use of the online system.

References:

Snelson, P. (1993). Relationships between access and use in informations systems: Remote access to and browsing of online catalogs. Proceedings of the 56th Annual Meeting of the American Society for Information Science, Columbus, Ohio, October 24-28, 1993. Medford, NJ: Learned Information, Inc.

Snelson, P. (1994). Remote users of OPAC's: Do they differ from library users? Proceedings 1994 - Integrated Online Library Systems Ninth National Conference. New York, May 11-12, 1994. Medford, NJ: Learned Information, Inc.

1.1 Please indicate your affiliation with Drew by entering a number from the following list:

1.Student   2.Faculty   3.Staff   4.Other

1.2 What is your department or major?

_____

2. Terminal Access:

Please indicate for the following pair of words your feelings about your ACCESS TO OAK by entering a number from 1 to 5 at the prompt.

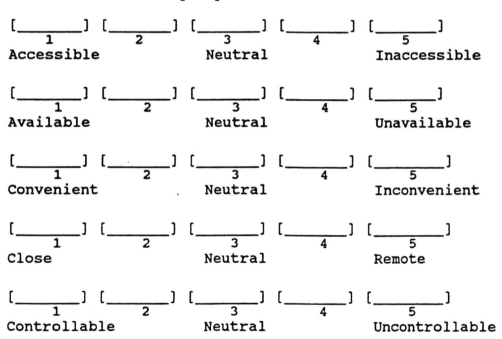

```
[_____] [_____] [_____] [_____] [_____]
     1          2          3          4          5
Accessible            Neutral              Inaccessible


[_____] [_____] [_____] [_____] [_____]
     1          2          3          4          5
Available            Neutral              Unavailable


[_____] [_____] [_____] [_____] [_____]
     1          2          3          4          5
Convenient           Neutral              Inconvenient


[_____] [_____] [_____] [_____] [_____]
     1          2          3          4          5
Close                Neutral              Remote


[_____] [_____] [_____] [_____] [_____]
     1          2          3          4          5
Controllable         Neutral              Uncontrollable
```

3. Source Access:

Please indicate for the following pair of words your feelings about OAK based on your USE OF OAK by entering a number from 1 to 5 at the prompt.

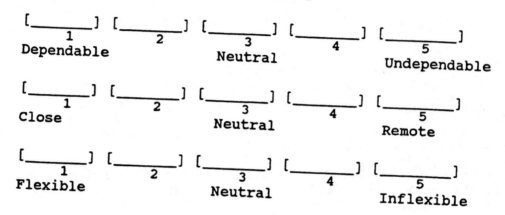

[_____] [_____] [_____] [_____] [_____]
    1   2   3   4   5
Dependable   Neutral   Undependable

[_____] [_____] [_____] [_____] [_____]
    1   2   3   4   5
Close   Neutral   Remote

[_____] [_____] [_____] [_____] [_____]
    1   2   3   4   5
Flexible   Neutral   Inflexible

4. Frequency:

4.1. In the last month, how many times did you use OAK from your DORM ROOM, OFFICE OR HOME? _____

4.2. In the last month, how many times did you use OAK while IN THE LIBRARY? _____

5. Task Variety:

Why did you use OAK today? Using the following list enter the letters of ALL reasons that apply (all on one line).

a. Recreational uses

b. Class or course reading

c. A thesis or dissertation

d. Teaching or planning a course

e. Keeping up to date on a topic or subject

f. Personal interest

g. A course paper or report

h. Writing for publication

i. Other

6. Effectiveness:

6.1 On a scale from 1 to 5, indicate the degree to which the information you found was of value or utility to the purpose of your search.

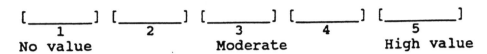

```
[_____] [_____] [_____] [_____] [_____]
    1          2          3          4          5
No value              Moderate              High value
```

6.2 On a scale from 1 to 5, to what extent did you find what you were looking for?

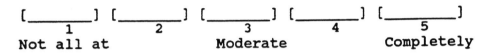

```
[_____] [_____] [_____] [_____] [_____]
    1          2          3          4          5
Not all at            Moderate              Completely
```

6.3 On a scale from 1 to 5, how satisfied in general were you with the completeness of your search results?

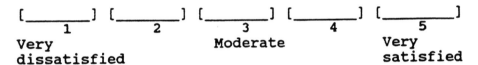

```
[_____] [_____] [_____] [_____] [_____]
    1          2          3          4          5
Very                  Moderate              Very
dissatisfied                                satisfied
```

6.4. On a scale from 1 to 5, to what degree was the retrieved information serendipitous for you, i.e., finding unexpected, interesting information while looking for something else?

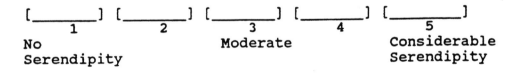

```
[_____] [_____] [_____] [_____] [_____]
    1          2          3          4          5
No                    Moderate              Considerable
Serendipity                                 Serendipity
```

HELP US EVALUATE THE NEW MENU SYSTEM

During Spring Break, menu access was added to our library workstations. LaserCat, Academic Abstracts, E. G. White Writings, and ERIC (CD-ROM products) can all be accessed from any of the five Lobby or two South Reading Room networked library computers. Please let us know how well the new system meets your needs. Also, let us know what CD-ROMs you'd like to see on the network.

Status: _____ Student _____ Grad Student _____ Faculty _____ Staff _____ Community member

		Strongly Somewhat	Agree Disagree	Neither Agree or Somewhat	Disagree Strongly	Disagree	Agree
1.	Overall, the new menu is easy to use:	_____	_____	_____	_____	_____	
2.	Help screens provided valuable information:	_____	_____	_____	_____	_____	
3.	I needed some personal assistance to exit the individual products and return to the main menu:	_____	_____	_____	_____	_____	
4.	I prefer the old system where there was one product per workstation:	_____	_____	_____	_____	_____	
5.	I was able to print satisfactorily the results of my search:	_____	_____	_____	_____	_____	

6. I would like to see the following CD-Rom resources on the network. My priority order is indicated by 1 being highest priority and 10 being lowest:

_____ Reader's Guide   _____ Social Science Index   _____ Business Periodicals Index

_____ Humanities Index   _____ encyclopedia or dictionary   _____ Biological and Agricultural Index

_____ Applied Science & Technology Index   _____ index devoted to computer science

_____ other: _____

For the 1993-1994 school year there will be limited funding for new periodical titles. List one title to which you would like to see the library subscribe (give full title and as much other information as possible).

Comments:

Faculty FirstSearch Evaluation Form

Feinberg Library is testing the FirstSearch information system as part of a SUNY-wide pilot project. Your input on this form will help us decide what we do with FirstSearch in the future. We thank you for your participation.

===

Please rate the FirstSearch system on the following criteria. Circle the number that most nearly expresses your rating on the scale provided.

1. Which databases did you search most often (see appended list)

_____

2. Coverage of information in FirstSearch important to your discipline:

    1   2   3   4   5

    (1=very useful; 3=useful; 5=not useful)

3. Usefulness of FirstSearch for undergraduate research:

    (1=very useful; 3=useful; 5=not useful)

    1   2   3   4   5

4. How easy was it to use FirstSearch?

    1   2   3   4   5

    (1=very easy; 3=easy; 5=very difficult)

5. If you had problems, how did you find help?
   ___ I used the online HELP function
   ___ I asked a colleague for help
   ___ I used an instructional handout/guide
   ___ I contacted the Library for help
   ___ I did not find help

6. How useful was the information you found in FirstSearch?

    1   2   3   4   5

    (1=very useful; 3=useful; 5=not useful)

7. How easy was it to use FirstSearch to print your search results?

1   2   3   4   5

(1=very easy; 3=easy; 5=very difficult)

8. How satisfied were you with FirstSearch?

1   2   3   4   5

(1=very satisfied; 3=satisfied; 5=very dissatisfied)

9. Describe any special features of FirstSearch that seem especially valuable in facilitating research:

_____

_____

_____

10. Other comments on FirstSearch:

_____

_____

_____

Surveys on Specific Areas or Services of the Library

St. Olaf College
: An effort to measure the impact of bibliographic instruction.

Mary Washington College
: A survey on interlibrary loan services.

St. John Fisher College
: A survey on technical services, done in a two-step process.

St. Olaf College

Library Bibliographic Instruction Survey

1. **Class:**   1 First year   2 Sophomore   3 Junior   4 Senior   5 Special student

2. **Has a librarian ever visited one of your classes (i.e. presented a bibliographic instruction [BI] session)?**   1 Yes   2 No

[CIRCLE ALL THAT APPLY.]

3. Where did you learn about the following? (Circle all that apply.)	In a BI session	Asked a Reference Librarian	Other library worker	My Prof.	Figured it out myself	Not a relevant tool	Don't know about
a. Scholarly Subject Encyclopedias and Dictionaries [e.g. *Encyclopedia of the Holocaust, Interpreter's Dictionary of the Bible,* etc.]	1	2	3	4	5	6	7
b. Thesauri [e.g. *Lib. of Congress Subject Headings, Thesaurus of Psychological Index Terms*]	1	2	3	4	5	6	7
c. Subject Bibliographies	1	2	3	4	5	6	7
d. PALS: St. Olaf Catalog	1	2	3	4	5	6	7
Other PALS Indexes [e.g. *GPO, EAI, ERI*]	1	2	3	4	5	6	7
e. Journal Indexes: Print [e.g. paper volumes of *Social Sciences Index, Humanities Index,* etc.]	1	2	3	4	5	6	7
Electronic [e.g. computer versions versions of *Psyclit, Sociofile,* etc.]	1	2	3	4	5	6	7
f. Interlibrary loan	1	2	3	4	5	6	7
g. Choosing relevant reference tools such as those listed above	1	2	3	4	5	6	7
h. Evaluating whether the sources I find (books, articles, manuscripts, etc.) are relevant to the field in which I'm doing research.	1	2	3	4	5	6	7
i. Evaluating the authority of sources I find (books, articles, manuscripts, etc.) and determining if they are accurate, reliable, and accepted by the scholarly community.	1	2	3	4	5	6	7

4. How do you rate your ability to use/do the following?	Very comfortable	Somewhat comfortable	Somewhat uncomfortable	Very uncomfortable/ Don't know how to use
a. Scholarly Subject Encyclopedias and Dictionaries [e.g. *Encyclopedia of the Holocaust, Interpreter's Dictionary of the Bible,* etc.]	1	2	3	4
b. Thesauri [e.g. *Library of Congress Subject Headings, Thesaurus of Psychological Index Terms*]	1	2	3	4
c. Subject Bibliographies	1	2	3	4
d. PALS: St. Olaf Catalog	1	2	3	4
Other PALS Indexes [e.g. *GPO, EAI, ERI*]	1	2	3	4
e. Journal Indexes: Print [e.g. paper volumes of *Social Sciences Index, Humanities Index,* etc.]	1	2	3	4
Electronic [e.g. computer versions of *Psyclit, Sociofile,* etc.]	1	2	3	4
f. Interlibrary loan	1	2	3	4
g. Choosing relevant reference tools such as those listed above	1	2	3	4
h. Evaluating whether the sources I find (books, articles, manuscripts, etc.) are relevant to the field in which I'm doing research.	1	2	3	4
i. Evaluating the authority of sources I find (books, articles, manuscripts, etc.), and determining if they are accurate, reliable, and accepted by the scholarly community.	1	2	3	4

[OVER]

5. In which year(s) did you have a BI session?   1 First year   2 Sophomore   3 Junior   4 Senior

For which course(s)?	1st course:	_____
		Course name	Instructor	Department
	2nd course:	_____
		Course name	Instructor	Department
	3rd course:	_____
		Course name	Instructor	Department
	4th course:	_____
		Course name	Instructor	Department

6. IF YOU HAVE TAKEN A BI SESSION, how helpful was your session in: [1st course]	Very helpful	Somewhat helpful	Of very little help	Not at all helpful
a. conducting your research for the course in in which you took it?	1	2	3	4
b. doing research in other courses?	1	2	3	4
c. allowing you to use your library research time more efficiently?	1	2	3	4
d. revealing where/who to ask for further assistance?	1	2	3	4
IF YOU HAVE TAKEN A BI SESSION, how helpful was your session in: [2nd course]				
a. conducting your research for the course in in which you took it?	1	2	3	4
b. doing research in other courses?	1	2	3	4
c. allowing you to use your library research time more efficiently?	1	2	3	4
d. revealing where/who to ask for further assistance?	1	2	3	4

7. If there are areas of bibliographic research in which you did not receive instruction, but wished you had, what are they?

8. What about the research process is most confusing for you? (We are interested in the process rather than specific sources.)

9. Which parts of the research process have become clearer as the result of a BI session? (We are interested in the process rather than specific sources.)

INTERLIBRARY LOAN

The interlibrary loan service obtains books, articles, dissertations, and other materials that the Simpson Library does not own for MWC students, faculty and staff.

1. *Have you ever used interlibrary loan at the Simpson Library?*

    ❑ Yes   ❑ No   *If you answered NO, please skip to question 14.*

2. *How many times have you used interlibrary loan during the 1994-95 school year?*

    ❑ 0-3 times   ❑ 4-6 times   ❑ 7-9 times   ❑ 10 or more times

3. *If you obtained an article, how would you rate the quality of the photocopy?*

    ❑ Excellent   ❑ Good   ❑ Fair   ❑ Poor   ❑ Never obtained an article

4. *Would you be interested in receiving interlibrary loan articles on a floppy disc?*

    ❑ Yes   ❑ No   ❑ Don't know enough to answer

5. *Would you be interested in receiving interlibrary loan articles via your e-mail account?*

    ❑ Yes   ❑ No   ❑ Don't know enough to answer

6. *How would you prefer to be notified that your interlibrary loan has arrived?*

    ❑ Campus mail ❑ Telephone   ❑ E-mail   ❑ Other _____

7. *Where do you usually find the citations for your interlibrary loan requests?*

    ❑ CD-ROM print-out   ❑ Print indexes   ❑ Bibliography in article or book
    ❑ *DIALOG* search   ❑ *FirstSearch*   ❑ Saw in another library
    ❑ Faculty recommendation

8. *Have you ever had to pay for an interlibrary loan you requested?*

    ❑ Yes   ❑ No

9. *How would you rate the time it took to receive your interlibrary loan?*

    ❑ Excellent   ❑ Good   ❑ Fair   ❑ Poor

3

10. *What is the longest amount of time you have had to wait for an interlibrary loan?*

    ❑ 1 week   ❑ 2 weeks   ❑ 3 weeks   ❑ 4 weeks or longer

    What is the shortest amount of time you have had to wait for an interlibrary loan?

    ❑ 1-3 days   ❑ 4-6 days   ❑ 7-10 days   ❑ 11 days or longer

11. *In what disciplines (Biology, English, History, etc.) do you find yourself having to use the interlibrary loan service the most?*

    _____

12. *Have you ever had your interlibrary loan request form returned to you?*

    ❑ No   ❑ Yes _____ times

    If YES, why was it returned?
    - ❑ Incomplete ILL form
    - ❑ Incorrect citation (title of book, author, etc.)
    - ❑ Library was unable to locate item
    - ❑ Request could not be processed by last date needed
    - ❑ Other (specify) _____

13. *The library does not charge for interlibrary loans in most cases. Would you be willing to pay (generally $15 - $20) for faster turnaround time for copies of articles?*

    ❑ Yes   ❑ No   ❑ In certain circumstances

> *Please answer questions 14-15 only if you have NOT used interlibrary loan.*

---

14. *Why have you not used the interlibrary loan service?*

    - ❑ I can usually find the resources I need available at the Simpson Library.
    - ❑ The service takes too long for my research needs.
    - ❑ I may have to pay a fee for articles.
    - ❑ I did not know about the interlibrary loan service.
    - ❑ I am not an MWC student, faculty, or staff member.
    - ❑ The request form is difficult to fill out (feel free to comment on next page).
    - ❑ Other (specify) _____

15. *Do you foresee yourself using interlibrary loan in the future?*

    ❑ Yes   ❑ No   ❑ Don't know

4

COMMENTS

Additional comments you would like to make about the library, interlibrary loan, or this survey.

_____

_____

_____

_____

_____

_____

Do you foresee the network installation significantly changing the role and/or services the library provides? If so, how?

_____

_____

_____

_____

_____

Date _____   *Time* _____ *A.M.* _____ *P.M.* _____

5

LIBRARY TECHNICAL SERVICES SURVEY

The Technical Services Department of the Library is in the process of examining its service to the faculty. We have designed this short survey to learn what you expect of us. A later survey will ask if we are meeting, exceeding, or falling short of your expectations. The end result of this process will be improvements in the way we support your work as teaching faculty. Thank you in advance for taking the time to give us your comments.

In case you are not sure what we do, let us explain that the Technical Services Department performs three main functions:

Acquisitions -

Working with the faculty, all types of library materials are selected, ordered, received, paid for, and weeded to provide a useful collection for our patrons.

Cataloging -

Materials are described, classified, and recorded to allow patrons to find information efficiently.

Processing -

Materials are physically prepared, labelled, preserved, and repaired so that patrons can locate and use them.

1) Please check any and all of the following services you want or need. This list includes projected as well as current services.

___ Publishers' information about new titles
___ Reviews of new titles
___ Topical bibliographies of potential purchases
___ Suggestions for departmental purchases
___ Monthly reports of departmental expenditures
___ Price and availability information about titles
___ Other

2) When you request materials for library purchase, do you want or need (check all that apply):

___ Notification that the item was or was not ordered?
___ Notification of changes in the status of a request/order (not yet published, back ordered, etc.)?
___ Notification that the material is ready to use?
___ Other?

LIBRARY - TECHNICAL SERVICES SURVEY
"Second Edition"

Thank you so much for your responses to the "first edition" of our survey! As promised, we are now giving you an opportunity to tell us how we are doing.

Please take a few minutes to answer the questions below. **Keep in mind that all answers apply to the Technical Services Department (acquisitions, cataloging, processing) only.**

Circle the number representing your response.

1 = Always	2 = Usually	3 = Sometimes	4 = Never

Technical Services provides helpful material
on prospective library purchases. 1 2 3 4 N/A

I am notified of the progress of my requests. 1 2 3 4 N/A

The monthly list of new acquisitions is useful to me. 1 2 3 4 N/A

I look at the new book display. 1 2 3 4 N/A

Items I have requested are ready for me to use
when I need them. 1 2 3 4 N/A

Adequate information is available about the
audio visual collection. 1 2 3 4 N/A

The library collection supports my courses
adequately. 1 2 3 4 N/A

My questions are answered completely and
competently. 1 2 3 4 N/A

When the library is automated, I will continue
to use the card catalog. 1 2 3 4 N/A

Comments: _____

_____

_____

_____

_____

Thank you so much for your participation! Please return surveys to
Library - Technical Services by Monday, April 27, 1992.

KJ 4/15/92

- 2 -

3) How soon after materials are requested (NON-RUSH titles) do you expect to see them on the shelf, ready to use?

___ Within 2 weeks   ___ Within 6 months
___ Within 2 months   ___ Speed is not usually important

4) Do you feel that our catalogs, files, and lists are easy to use to locate materials in this library?

___ Yes ___ No   Suggestions for improvement? _____
_____
_____

5) Please comment on the physical condition of our materials:

Books: ___ Good ___ Fair ___ Poor
Periodicals: ___ Good ___ Fair ___ Poor
Audio-Visuals: ___ Good ___ Fair ___ Poor
Suggestions for improvement? _____
_____
_____

6) Please comment on the courtesy, friendliness and attitude of the Technical Services staff.

___ Excellent   ___ Needs improvement
___ Average   ___ Cannot comment

7) Is there anything more our department can do to support and assist you in your work? Please specify.

_____
_____
_____

8) Have you ever had any contact with our department?

___ Yes ___ No

Please return this completed form via campus mail to Library Technical Services by April 1, 1992. (No connection with April Fool's Day!)

3/23/92 KJ

Facilities Surveys

Sweet Briar College
Excerpted from a longer survey, this section solicits input from users as part of a planning process for a new building.

University of the South
A very focused survey on what type of study space students prefer.

Monday, April 6, 1992

	Adequate	Inadequate	No Comment
Library seating and study space	☐	☐	☐

Comments:

_____
_____
_____
_____
_____
_____
_____

Library access (steps, elevators, etc.)	☐	☐	☐

Comments:

_____
_____
_____
_____
_____
_____
_____

List your major desires for library, e.g. more books, more periodicals, longer hours, more staff, additional computer databases, etc.)

_____
_____
_____
_____
_____
_____
_____

Some facilities could be associated with the libraries. For each one listed below, please indicate whether you feel Sweet Briar would benefit from having the facility located in the library.

Meeting Rooms

    Beneficial to include in library   ☐

    Not beneficial to include in library   ☐

    No opinion   ☐

Group Study Rooms

    Beneficial to include in library   ☐

    Not beneficial to include in library   ☐

    No opinion   ☐

Monday, April 6, 1992

Private Carrels
    Beneficial to include in library ❑
    Not beneficial to include in library ❑
    No opinion ❑

Audio Listening Rooms
    Beneficial to include in library ❑
    Not beneficial to include in library ❑
    No opinion ❑

Video Viewing Rooms
    Beneficial to include in library ❑
    Not beneficial to include in library ❑
    No opinion ❑

Lecture Rooms
    Beneficial to include in library ❑
    Not beneficial to include in library ❑
    No opinion ❑

Small Seminar Rooms
    Beneficial to include in library ❑
    Not beneficial to include in library ❑
    No opinion ❑

Children's Library
    Beneficial to include in library ❑
    Not beneficial to include in library ❑
    No opinion ❑

Faculty Offices
    Beneficial to include in library ❑
    Not beneficial to include in library ❑
    No opinion ❑

Video Editing facility
    Beneficial to include in library ❑
    Not beneficial to include in library ❑
    No opinion ❑

Computer Lab
    Beneficial to include in library ❏
    Not beneficial to include in library ❏
    No opinion ❏

Closed Book Stacks
    Beneficial to include in library ❏
    Not beneficial to include in library ❏
    No opinion ❏

Open Book Stacks
    Beneficial to include in library ❏
    Not beneficial to include in library ❏
    No opinion ❏

Closed Journal Stacks
    Beneficial to include in library ❏
    Not beneficial to include in library ❏
    No opinion ❏

Open Journal Stacks
    Beneficial to include in library ❏
    Not beneficial to include in library ❏
    No opinion ❏

Drive up Book Return
    Beneficial to include in library ❏
    Not beneficial to include in library ❏
    No opinion ❏

Outdoor Seating for reading and study
    Beneficial to include in library ❏
    Not beneficial to include in library ❏
    No opinion ❏

Rare Book, Archives & Museum Exhibition area
    Beneficial to include in library ❏
    Not beneficial to include in library ❏
    No opinion ❏

Monday, April 6, 1992

Storage facility for little used materials
    Beneficial to include in library ☐
    Not beneficial to include in library ☐
    No opinion ☐

Certain campus facilities either are, have been or could be associated with the libraries. For each one listed below, please indicate whether you feel Sweet Briar would benefit from having the facility located in the library.

Media Services
    Beneficial to include in library ☐
    Not beneficial to include in library ☐
    No opinion ☐

Microcomputer Services
    Beneficial to include in library ☐
    Not beneficial to include in library ☐
    No opinion ☐

Academic Resource Center (ARC)
    Beneficial to include in library ☐
    Not beneficial to include in library ☐
    No opinion ☐

Language Laboratory
    Beneficial to include in library ☐
    Not beneficial to include in library ☐
    No opinion ☐

Duplicating
    Beneficial to include in library ☐
    Not beneficial to include in library ☐
    No opinion ☐

Other (Please Specify)

_____
_____
_____
_____
_____
_____
_____

Survey - Student Seating in the Library

We are trying to assess the effectiveness of study space in the library so that we can better provide the types of space you prefer for studying. Please take a moment to complete this survey and return it in confidence to: Annie Armour-Jones, Archives, duPont Library
Thank You

1. I study in the library:

____ more than four hours per week
____ 1-4 hours per week
____ less than one hour per week

2. I best describe my library study patterns **one** of the following ways (library study space is in the form of open tables, carrels, offices, quiet study, group study, and computer access study):

____ I use library study space for most of my work
____ I use library study space mostly to study for tests
____ I use library study space mostly for writing papers
____ I use library study space when I must use materials that do not circulate
____ I don't use the library to study

3. I use the following types of study space: (on a scale of 1-4, 4 means mostly, 3 means sometimes, 2 means seldom, and 1 means never):

____ closed carrels
____ open carrels
____ open tables for individual study
____ open tables for group study
____ open tables for reference research

____ open lounge areas
____ group study rooms
____ quiet study
____ I try to find an empty room for studying
____ I prefer the night study atmosphere, with all the study tables together

____ I look for the most private place I can find
____ I do not mind traffic when I study
____ I prefer studying near a window
____ I prefer studying with other people
____ I need computer access

____ I like to study in small groups with computer access
____ I need a space with multi-media access
____ I like studying in the balcony area above the reading room
____ I'd like to read in the lobby

____ I study in my room
____ I use the new after hours study room in Woods Lab
____ I use other buildings on campus for studying

4. I am a:
____ Freshman
____ Sophomore
____ Junior
____ Senior

Focus Groups and Interviews

Ohio Wesleyan University
A carefully constructed script for focus groups on bibliographic instruction, consisting of groups of faculty and students who had and had not participated in BI. Suggestions and excerpt from the library's annual report also noteworthy.

Wheelock College
As part of a self-study, a survey, interviews, and focus groups were used. Included here is an account of the procedure and the interview questions used.

William Paterson College
A focus group of faculty was recorded and analyzed in order to develop questions for a subsequent survey on audiovisual services.

Focus Group Interview Questions

<u>Faculty Groups</u>
A. Faculty Who Request Librarian-Assisted BI
1. What is your general opinion of the value of the OWU Libraries bibliographic instruction program? From what you have seen of your students' efforts, does their work reflect a gain derived from library instruction?

2. Do you feel that most of your students come into your courses with satisfactory library skills? Please cite examples supporting and opposing this contention.

3. What is your perception of how your students accept library instruction? Do they understand its purpose? Do you think they see it as being of value or just busy work?

4. Do the bibliographic instruction offered by the librarians fulfill your expectations for your students? If not, why and how might they be improved?

5. In what ways would you suggest that the program be revised and improved in order to become a more meaningful experience for your students? Can material during the classroom sessions be presented in a manner that holds the students interest as well as teaching them something of substance, that is, is any type of format change in order? Would self-paced, programmed instruction by means of a workbook or a set of library research exercises meet the needs of some or all of your students? Would computer-aided instruction be of value? Do you think it possible to identify the learning styles of your students so that bibliographic instruction might be offered to them in a format from which they would profit most? Is the latter statement a realistic expectation within the time frame of a semester?

6. Are there other comments or suggestions you would like to make about the bibliographic instruction program?

B. Faculty Who Have Not Used Librarian-Assisted BI
1. Even though you usually do not use bibliographic instruction with your students, the librarians certainly appreciate your willingness to lend your time and your ideas to this study. To begin do you believe that your students come into your courses with sufficient skill in using the library? Does their work results reflect adequate library skills? Are they meeting your expectations for the library research that you require?

2. Is formal or informal instruction in the use of the library's resources and services a valid utilization of librarian time?

3. Do you believe that it is your responsibility in teaching your students how to use the library? Have you ever considered asking

Focus Groups, page 2

a librarian to assist you in teaching your class about the library?

4. What is your opinion of student learning styles? Is it possible to address individual learning styles during the course of semester? Do you believe that library instruction might benefit from attempting to address each student's learning style?

5. In what ways do you see that your students might benefit from a bibliographic instruction session? Would alternative learning strategies such as programmed self-instruction by means of a workbook and computer-aided instruction be advantageous?

6. What other comments or suggestions do you have that might help in the revision of the bibliographic instruction program?

Student Groups
A. Freshmen Who Were in English 12 Classes During the Past Semester
1. Having just completed English 12, you were involved in several exercises aimed at familiarizing you with the O.W.U. Library system and how to utilize its resources and services for class assignments. Before enrolling, what was your assessment of your capability in using libraries?

2. During the library sessions offered in conjunction with your English 12 class, what did you learn that was new to you in regards to using libraries?

3. Did you find the material covered in these sessions useful in fulfilling your class assignments, or did it seem like mostly busy work?

4. Was having information about the library presented in a classroom setting helpful or not? Did the librarian present the material in way that was clear and easy to understand? Were the important points in these sessions made evident? Was the use of teaching aids such as overhead transparencies, paper handouts, and viewing searches of LS/2000 through an enlarged image helpful in enabling you to know what was important? If you found these classroom sessions of little help, how might they be improved?

5. How do you learn best? Of the different types of learning experiences you have had in your academic career, which have been most useful and beneficial? Do you believe that the library material can be presented to you effectively by another means other than in the classroom? Would viewing a video, using a computer program, or completing a workbook of exercises covering the same information covered in the library classroom sessions accomplish the same goals? Which of those options mentioned above seem most appealing to you? Does the classroom setting offer any advantages over the three possibilities for self-paced learning? Would setting up an appointment with a librarian for a

Focus Group Questions, page 3

one-on-one session much of the same material have value?

6. Do you feel that some form of introduction to the library with its collections, resources, and services is a necessary part of your educational experience at O.W.U.? What general or overall improvements would you suggest in the library instruction program? If you do not believe that this program is of much value, should it be abandoned?

B. Students in Upper Division Classes for which the Instructor Requested Librarian-Assisted BI
1. You have taken classes in which the professor asked a librarian to meet with the class to go over library sources and services that were of particular relevance to an assignment. Did you find such a library-related session helpful to your work in that course?

2. Tell what else you recall about library sessions for the courses that you have taken so far. Does anything standout in terms of what you learned or what the librarian disclosed or demonstrated? Given your own familiarity with using the O.W.U. Library system, do you believe you could find the information discussed in the classroom session on your own? Have the library sessions in which you have participated been an asset or not?

3. Was the librarian effective in explaining the information relevant to that session? Can you imagine ways in which the information may have been presented better?

4. How or in what manner do you learn best? Is a classroom presentation the most effective setting for supplementary library sessions? Do you think a video, computer program, or printed workbook (for self-paced instruction) could cover the same material just as well if not better? What is your opinion of making an appointment with a librarian for a private, one-to-one session covering the same subject matter? Does such a one-to-one session offer advantages over the other forms of library instruction previously described?

6. In general do you have any other suggestions for how to improve the library instruction program in relation to presentations geared to specific course assignments? Or are you of the mind that such sessions are of marginal value and should be discontinued?

C. Students who have very seldom or never participated in bibliographic instruction sessions.
1. First, let me thank you for taking the time to take part in this study. Do not be concerned about what you do or do not know. You are not being evaluated on your answers. Rather, a candid, free exchange of your ideas about the coming questions will assist the librarians significantly in their efforts to make

Focus Groups, page 4

learning about the library a useful and meaningful aspect of your education. First, tell me what has been your past experience in using libraries. When you arrived at Ohio Wesleyan, what was your initial impression of the library system? Did you find that your knowledge of libraries from secondary school or from using the public library in your community adequate for using the library resources here?

2. Did your English 12 class take part in library instruction sessions? Did your English 12 instructor take time to personally teach you about how to find information in the library? Do you believe that you learned enough about using the library resources on campus in English 12 so that you have been able to perform the required research for other courses?

3. Are you of the opinion that knowing how to access the resources of the library system is an important part of your college education? If not, please explain why. Do you feel that you are able to meet sufficiently the requirements of your courses without prepared instruction in the use of the library? If you agree that the latter statement is correct, is that due to the nature of your course of study (i.e., some fields of study require more library research than others), or is that a conclusion you have reached due to your own experience?

4. At this point in your education, do you feel reasonably sure about how you best learn, or how do you learn most effectively? Do you think that if library instruction were offered in some form other than a classroom presentation, could yourself and others gain more from it? If library instruction were offered in the form of a self-paced workbook of exercises, a video presentation, a computer program, or a one-to-one session with a librarian, do any of these options sound more attractive or beneficial in terms of investing the time?

5. At this point, do you believe that you will be doing or need to know how to do research on a wide variety of subjects after completing your college education? If your answer is yes, do you think that the information will be found in a small number of familiar sources or in numerous sources some of which you may never knew existed? If your answer is no, what brought you to that conclusion?

6. Do you understand the meaning of the phrase "lifelong learner"? If you do, would you use it to describe yourself? Do you see a role for libraries to play in the lifelong learning process? If you believe that libraries do have a role in lifelong learning, what examples can you give?

7. At this point, can you offer any other suggestions of what the library system might do in order to improve its program of library instruction? Or do you consider library instruction an

Focus Groups, page 5

unnecessary activity that should be discontinued?

D. Seniors about to Graduate
1. As you look back over your college career, how many times can you recall that you were involved in some formal library instruction activity? Were those instances you can recall in English 12 or in other courses in relation to a specific assignment?

2. Do you believe that a thorough knowledge of the library system's resources and how to access them is an integral part of a college education? Do you think a knowledge of library resources and the means to access these sources will be of value as your life moves beyond the campus?

3. What is your interpretation of the phrase, "lifelong learner?" Do you believe that this phrase can be applied to you? If you think you understand and support this concept, how might you put it into practice in the future? Do libraries have any role to play in the lifelong learning process?

4. At this point in your college career, do you believe that you know what learning styles work best for you? Have library instruction sessions in which you have been involved been conducted in a competent manner? Do you recall if the information imparted during the library sessions was useful as well as interesting? Do you believe that other means of instruction in library use may be of merit such as using a self-paced workbook of library exercises, viewing a video about the library, using a computer program that teaches one about the library, or extensive one-to-one sessions with a librarian? Do you think you may have gained more if one of the above options had been available to you?

5. Do any of your experiences in library instruction sessions stand out in your memory in a positive or negative light? If some do, please explain why.

6. Overall, what suggestions might you propose to improve the quality of library instruction on this campus? Or do you believe that instruction in the use of the library collections and their means of access is of marginal value and should be abandoned?

Focus Groups, page 6

E. Students Trained on Electronic Information Retrieval Systems
1. You have participated in a training session for the Classmate online information system, the PsychLit database, or some government document database held by the library on compact disk. Were these training sessions the first in which you had taken part in an instructional exercise sponsored and conducted by the Ohio Wesleyan University library system? If they were not, in what other library-sponsored activities have you been involved? If they were your first, do you think they were successful in presenting and describing how to access the information you were seeking?

2. What was your opinion of how the librarian leading the session presented the subject matter? Was the material offered explained in a clear and understandable manner? Did the librarian demonstrate a mastery of the material? Did he or she provide sufficient time for members of your group to ask questions? At the end of the session, did you feel confident and able to use the electronic database system? What improvements might you suggest for this type of research training?

3. How do you see such library instructional opportunities fitting into your education at Ohio Wesleyan in general? Do you believe that library instruction is a valuable part of a college education? Why or why not? Can one receive a solid educational experience with minimal or no library skills? If the electronic database training has been your only contact with the library instructional program, can see ways in which other library instruction activities might benefit students? Now are there other aspects about using the library about which you wish to know? Can you offer suggestions about how the library instruction program can be offered in the most meaningful way to students?

SUGGESTED CHANGES FROM FACULTY

DEVELOP HANDOUTS & SELF-INSTRUCTION
1. Provide students with an "owner's manual to the library" (B)
2. Need manual for CLASSMATE (B)
3. Design flow charts of search process (B)

BI CONTENT/FORMAT ISSUES
1. EN 12 with 4 library-related sessions too much, 2 sessions better (B)
2. Students need help using LC classification system (B)
3. Students need help using periodicals (B)
4. Concern with students who exempt out of EN 12 (B, W)
5. Library sessions by discipline for periodicals and papers (B)
6. Library sessions are too general (B)
7. Offer a course in research (B)

QUALITY OF STAFFING ISSUES
1. Librarians (no longer here) not properly prepared (W)
2. Librarians not much acquaintance in our field (B)
3. Choose liaisons for EN 12 (B)
4. Liaison should be proactive, do more than send CHOICE cards (W)
5. Have peer groups do library tours and info sessions (B)

PROMOTION OF LIBRARY
1. Liaisons should become better known to students (W)
2. Better publicity about online services: what's available, what's covered in workshops (B)
3. Publicize last days for ILL requests better (B)
4. Better publicity about AV services (B)

FOR FURTHER REFLECTION
What are the implications for the entire campus community that resources such as theatre's special collection, the slide library, and specialized periodicals in departments are located in places other than "the Library" (B)

(B) faculty with BI components
(W) non BI faculty

SUGGESTED CHANGES IN BI FROM STUDENTS

DEVELOP HANDOUTS & SELF-INSTRUCTION
1. Better instruction sheets (L)
2. Self-guided access to the resources (S)
3. A list of all the different types of sources you could go to, esp. by type of course or specific for major (N, S)
4. Prefer a manual for referencing what they don't know (F)
5. Instructional sheet or self-help manual for all types of things, CLASSMATE, OCLC, govt docs, librarians' hours, map (C)
6. Information (handbook, manual) about library mailed to all students (L, W)

IDEAS FOR IMPROVING THE BI PROGRAM
1. During orientation of new students, talk about resources of library not just LS2K (N, F)
2. Orientation should be available regularly, not just to new students (N)
3. EN 12 exempted students need library orientation (S, W)
4. More individual sessions --PsycLIT, Marcive (L)
5. Need to know more about the reference section (N)
6. Teach difference between Dewey and LC (W)
7. BI sessions oriented to the major (N, S)

IDEAS CONCERNING THE FORMAT OF BI
1. After one-on-one instruction, provide take home instructions (N)
2. Prefer one-on-one or small group (F)
3. Want small groups (5-6 members) (S); 25-30 is too big, recommend 8-10 (L)
4. Hands-on instruction important (S, C)
5. Need more hands-on experience with CLASSMATE (C, L)
6. Avoid "dry" lectures (S)
7. LS2K demo has too much detail (F)
8. Need to see where ref works are in the library (C)
9. Improve wording on self-guided tours (W)

PROMOTION OF BI PROGRAM
1. Publicize library liaisons (N, S)

(N) no BI students
(S) seniors
(F) freshman who had EN 12
(C) course-related BI
(L) library sponsored BI
(W) library student assistants

SUGGESTED CHANGES FOR OTHER AREAS OF THE LIBRARY
FROM STUDENTS

MATERIAL
1. Clean up lost books on LS2K (N)
2. Books are too dated (L), esp. Psychology (N)
3. More journals, only 3?! for nursing (S)
4. Suggest adding lazy boy chairs (C)

ORGANIZATION
1. Better signage (N)
2. A floor plan would be helpful (N)
3. In reference area indicate contents on shelving units (C)
4. Identify "incomplete" in union list of periodicals (C)
5. Specific journal names on ranges (C)
6. Don't like microfilm stored in boxes with magazines (C)
7. Library needs to be quieter, esp 2nd and 3rd floor (F)
8. Don't like Qs on 2nd floor, Ns on 3rd floor (C)

TRAINING
1. More helpful students working in New Science (N)
2. Improve assistance from student assistants in periodicals, especially help with microfilm (C)

SERVICES
1. ILL too slow (C)
2. Microfilm readers need to be in working order at all times (C)
3. Extend hours, especially later at night, of branches (L)

(N) no BI students
(S) seniors
(F) freshman who had EN 12
(C) course-related BI
(L) library sponsored BI
(W) library student assistants

FROM ANNUAL REPORT

Coordinator of Bibliographic Instruction Paul Burman successfully completed a focus group study of the bibliographic instruction program. Floyd Dickman, from the State Library, moderated eight focus groups. The composition of the six student groups included freshman who had completed English 12, seniors, library student assistants, students with upper division courses where library instruction was given, students who had attended library-sponsored training, and students who had not received any librarian-led instruction. One faculty group included those who used librarian-led instruction, another faculty group those who did not.

The following goals were identified to improve the library instruction program:

1. ensure that all students receive some form of librarian-led training about the library system's collections and services;

2. promote library awareness with student and faculty groups;

3. produce additional library finding aids;

4. improve signage to assist library users;

5. refine teaching techniques of librarians;

6. offer training in electronic resources;

7. train some library student assistants to be "student mentors."

BACKGROUND AND GOALS

During the spring semester of 1994, the Committee on Library and Information Resources (Attachment A), formed to evaluate information services at Wheelock College and address the Library and Information Resources Standard for the NEASC accreditation. Specific areas studied were the Library, Audio-Visual Department and Resource Center. The goals of the study were:

1. To evaluate quantitatively and qualitatively how well library and information services at Wheelock College are meeting student and faculty needs.

2. To determine how students and faculty are using these services.

3. To identify areas of strength and weakness.

4. To pinpoint priority areas for improvement.

5. To provide data for addressing the NEASC Standard on Library and Information Resources.

6. To provide directions for planning future library and information resources services at Wheelock College.

METHODOLOGY

The Committee decided from the outset of the study that we needed both quantitative and qualitative information in order to conduct a useful evaluation. Surveys and studies from other academic institutions were reviewed and considered as possible data collection models. We were somewhat surprised at the paucity and inadequacy of survey instruments and the limited number of models reported in the literature. The University of Michigan Study (1991) was the most complete, and it clearly had been a considerable project in terms of time and money.

To meet our needs, the Committee decided on the following model: A pencil and paper survey of students and faculty, followed by individual interviews and focus groups. We decided that this combination of methods would provide necessary statistical data and also allow for more in-depth study and clarification. In addition, the time and cost of conducting the study would be manageable within our means.

2

PROCEDURE

First, the Committee conducted the pencil and paper survey. Members of the Committee developed and piloted two survey instruments: one designed for students and one for faculty (see Attachment B). The survey was administered to a sample of Associate Degree students, all Sophomores, a stratified sample of Seniors (by major), and a stratified sample of Graduate students (by program). The sample was purposefully designed to capture a stratified sample of graduate students by distributing the survey to all classes that met on two alternate nights of the week. Sampling students in this way covered a wide range of programs. As for the undergraduates, we selected sophomores in order to capture a perspective of students who were in the process of learning to use resources and seniors because of their broader experience. Faculty distributed the surveys in their classes and collected them upon completion. In total, 412 students completed the survey: 54 A.S., 199 undergraduate, and 159 graduate. The faculty completed their surveys during Undergraduate and Graduate faculty meetings, with 47 surveys returned.

Second, the Committee developed questions for the individual interviews with attention to preliminary results from the surveys (see Attachment C for interview questions). One of the Library's evening reference librarians conducted the interviews. She audio recorded each interview and prepared summaries to incorporate in the evaluation. In total, 13 students from various levels (Sophomores, Juniors, Graduate, etc.), majors and programs and 7 faculty (Undergraduate and Graduate, Liberal Arts and Professional Studies, and full-time and part-time) participated in the interviews. A compilation of interview responses is also in Attachment C.

Finally, focus group sessions of students and faculty were conducted. Dr. Elizabeth Larkin (Assistant Professor at Wheelock) conducted the student session. Eight students, a

3

stratified sample of the student population, attended the session. The faculty session was lead by Dr. Sharon Bostick (Library Director, U.Mass/Boston) and was attended by a stratified sample of 9 faculty. The purpose of the sessions was to find out what each group considered to be their ideal library, and to determine how they viewed current library services and collections at Wheelock in relation to the ideal. Each group was assured that what they said would be held in confidence and that individual names would not be used in the final report. Group leaders taped each of their sessions. A transcription of the student focus group along with a summary of suggestions is located in Attachment D. Dr. Bostick's report on the faculty focus group is in Attachment E.

4

Interview Questions

1. Why do you/don't you use Wheelock's Library? (Either for your own research or to prepare for courses.)

    If you use it, what attracts you?

    If you don't use it is there something about it that keeps you away?

2. Which features are most positive of Wheelock's library services?

3. What frustrations have you experienced at the Library?

4. If you could improve one thing, what would it be?

5. As a student/faculty member, does Wheelock's Library meet your expectations for what a library should be? How so/how not?

6. How well does the collection and services of the Wheelock Library support your students' coursework and your research?

7. How well have we done in educating and informing you about our services?

8. What are your expectations of student staff? Is it clear which staff can answer what questions?

   If not how can we make this more clear?

9. Have you used the reserve system for your students? Please comment on your experiences.

10. Are journals available when you need them?

If not, what did you do?

11. Discuss your use of the A-V Center.

   Do you find enough help is available?

12. Do you have any other thoughts or comments regarding the Library and its collections and services?

<u>Instructions to Focus Group Participants</u>

Audiovisual Focus Group Format

<u>Introduction</u>

Thank you for coming to this focus group. The purpose of this focus group is to explore the effectiveness of past and present Audiovisual services provided by the library so that we may be more effective in the future. The way we would like to conduct this focus group is by allowing about five to ten minutes per topic area, followed by a brief survey. The topic areas will examine the past, present, and future of:

a) the role of audiovisual technology in the classroom;
b) the usefulness of different types of audiovisual technologies in the classroom;
c) the most effective delivery system of audiovisual technologies to the classroom; and
d) a general assessment the role, usefulness, and delivery effectiveness of audiovisual technology in the classroom;

We will proceed by asking you to react to each topic with whatever thoughts you have, based on your particular inclinations and experience. Your thoughts and ideas will shape what and how we deliver audiovisual services in the future, so we appreciate the time and attention you are giving us right now. We are recording this conversation so that we may transcribe and consider your reactions more closely later on, but please don't let that stop you from just speaking your mind.

My role, as moderator, is something like playing a therapist who is engaged in active, reflective listening: I will try to move the conversation forward only if we get stalled. And I will try to make sure we keep moving through the major topic areas. So, unless there are any questions, let's begin.

Moderator guidelines

Prompt #1: What AV technologies do you use?

1a. What have you used in the past?
1b. Do you have any sense of what is out there...What your choices are within the new technologies?
1c. Here's a list. Do you use any of these? Films...videos...slides...transparencies ...CD-ROM...interactive video...CD's...cassettes...?
1d. What does the future hold for us?
1e. Does any of this really help, or is it just sometimes expensive window dressing on the same ideas that can be taught in a conventional way?
1f. What are soem of the positive and negative characteristics of AV technologies?

Prompt #2: What do you believe should be the role of audiovisual technology in the classroom? How should such technologies be used?

2a. Do AV materials play a supplementary role?
2b. What has been AV's role in the past? the present? the future?
2c. Do you ever use it to play Devil's Advocate?
2d. What are we missing here? Is there some past, present, or future role for AV that we should be thinking of?
2e. Is convenience a major issue for you?
2f. Should the library be training students or faculty in the new technologies? Where should people be learning about these new technologies?

Prompt #3: How can the library help deliver these various technologies to students? How can the library help the most?

3a. What has your experience been as far getting equipment delivered to your classes?
3b. What about closed circuit TV or cable? Does anyone have any experience using that, or some other form of distance learning? Teleconferencing, E-mail, correspondence schools...
3c. In terms of everyday use, how important is convenience? Do you ever just "do a video" because you're tired, or rushed, or unprepared?
3d. What about special classrooms with particular technologies?
3e. What kinds of courses and departments are more likely to use the developing AV technologies?

Participant Survey

How important are AV technologies to your teaching and research activities, and how important do you believe they will be in the future? Please rate both the current and future (anticipated) importance of each of the following audiovisual related activities using a scale ranging from 0 (Least Important) through 9 (Most Important) or NA (Not Applicable).

IMPORTANCE TO TEACHING AND RESEARCH

	Current (0 through 9)	Future (0 through 9)

Type of Technology:

	Current	Future
Films	_____	_____
Videos	_____	_____
Slides	_____	_____
Transparencies	_____	_____
CD-ROM	_____	_____
Interactive video	_____	_____
CD's	_____	_____
Audiocassettes	_____	_____
Other:	_____	_____

Role of Technology:

	Current	Future
Supplement lecture	_____	_____
Supplement text	_____	_____
Primary source	_____	_____
Additional info.	_____	_____
"Devil's advocate"	_____	_____
Other:	_____	_____

How Technology is Delivered:

	Current	Future
Delivered to class	_____	_____
Cable/closed circuit TV	_____	_____
Computer exchanges	_____	_____
Teleconferencing	_____	_____
Correspondence	_____	_____
Dedicated Classrooms (computer labs, language labs)	_____	_____
Independent student workstations	_____	_____
Other:	_____	_____

Gender: M   F   Department:
Years teaching at college level: Years at WPC:
Primary focus (circle one): Teaching   Research   Service

Directions to Observers

Your task, as you listen to the recordings of these focus groups, is to non-judgmentally record what participants actually said. Use the accompanying sheet to indicate positive and negative comments made within each category, as well as any additional comments offered by participants. Then use the section at the bottom to indicate any other information you believe will be useful at trying to understand our participants reactions to the topics raised within these focus groups.

At the first stage, each of you should do this independently.

At the second stage, we will exchange and discuss what each has recorded, resolve differences whenever possible, and then create a summary report acknowledging any difference which may remain.

At the third stage, we will be able to transform this and quantitative information derived from the focus groups into a larger survey.

In the interests of time and convenience, it may be easiest to listen to the tapes together, working through stages 1 and 2 in one glorious marathon of interesting work. Just be sure not to discuss your initial assessment the first time through.

Observers: Please note comments made within each category. Focus group # ___

The Usefulness of Various Audiovisual Technologies in the Classroom

	Past +/-	Present +/-	Future +/-
Films			
Videos			
Slides			
Transparencies			
Multimedia (CD-ROM)			
Interactive video			
Audiocassettes, CD's, etc.			
Other (specify)			
Other (specify)			

Comments, Impressions, and Observations

William Paterson College

Observers: Please note comments made within each category Focus group # ___

The Role of Audiovisual Technology in the Classroom

	Past +/-	Present +/-	Future +/-
Supplement lecture			
Supplement text			
Primary Source			
Additional Information			
Comparative Information			
Other (specify):			
Other (specify):			

Comments, Impressions, and Observations

<u>Observers: Please note comments made within each category.</u> Focus group # ___

The Usefulness of Various Audiovisual
Technologies in the Classroom

	Past +/−	Present +/−	Future +/−

Films

Videos

Slides

Transparencies

Multimedia
(CD-ROM)

Interactive video

Audiocassettes, CD's, etc.

Other (specify)

Other (specify)

<u>Comments, Impressions, and Observations</u>

William Paterson College

A Survey and Needs Assessment
for the Audiovisual Department

of the

Sarah Byrd Askew Library,
William Paterson College of New Jersey

The Audiovisual (AV) Department of the Library is planning for our technology-rich future. Focus groups identified each of the items in this survey as a faculty concern regarding AV Distribution Services. Please note that your responses are confidential, but only at a personal level. We will be identifying what department and schools are represented by each response, as well as other general demographic information which will help us better understand who uses which types of audiovisual services the most frequently. The services and technologies provided by AV Distribution include distribution, set-up and delivery of overhead projectors, cassettes, films and videos, computers, CD-ROM, multimedia, and other emerging technologies.

This is an important planning document for the Library which will influence how we provide services. The scale takes about 10 minutes to complete. We sincerely thank you for your interest and cooperation.

A Survey and Needs Assessment for the Audiovisual Department

Use the scale to indicate your level of agreement with each of the following statements

1	2	3	4	5
<—				—>
Disagree		Neutral		Agree

General Awareness:

____ The AV Department has resources which can help my teaching.

____ My colleagues are generally aware of AV services and opportunities.

____ I did not even know that we had an AV Department, much less what they have to offer.

____ The AV Department is used extensively by some, but not all, departments.

Reputation:

____ The AV Department has never received the respect they deserve.

____ AV staff are quite capable.

____ The AV equipment frequently does not work.

____ I can never count on AV to get me the right thing at the right time.

____ I am satisfied with AV Distribution Services.

Public Relations:

____ I would like an AV rep. to visit my department with updated services about once a year.

____ I would like to know what the AV Department has to offer.

____ The AV Department should promote itself much more effectively.

____ I know most of what AV has to offer; I don't need more information.

____ I don't know what is available in my particular discipline.

Convenience:

____ In my experience, AV is very convenient.

____ Time is important. Usually, I can't obtain what I want from AV quickly enough.

____ Personal convenience, more than pedagogical practice, determines what I actually use.

____ AV materials are geographically inconvenient for me to obtain.

____ Convenience is important because it encourages spontaneity when I teach.

____ AV materials help me offer something of value when I am in a pinch.

____ To be effective, technology must be convenient for students as well as faculty.

Pedagogical Issues:

____ Use of videos and similar materials is as valid as conventional textbooks.

____ Technologies can help me teach my material more effectively.

____ Technologies can teach some material much better than conventional approaches.

____ AV is irrelevant because I don't have enough time to cover what I need to cover now.

____ AV technologies are not suited to my particular field.

____ Technologies are reshaping my field; we need to "get up to speed" quickly.

____ I can teach quite well without using new technologies.

Future Directions:

____ I am satisfied with the organizational structure of the AV Department within the college.

____ Current AV services are provided by too many different departments.

____ AV services should be decentralized into each academic building.

____ AV services should be decentralized into each academic school or department.

____ AV services are appropriately an exclusive function of the library.

____ AV services need to be linked to academic computing.

____ AV services should be provided by some single agency other than the library.

____ I anticipate needing more technology training in order to use AV materials.

Role:

_____ I would like AV to train me in the use of technologies applied to teaching.

_____ The AV role should emphasize responding to faculty rather than initiating change.

_____ The AV role is appropriately limited to supplying me with the equipment I need.

_____ AV staff are not professional instructors; they are support staff to professional instructors.

_____ The AV Department, not faculty, should be training students in new technologies.

_____ I would like AV to train me how to integrate media into my curriculum.

AV Technology in the Classroom:

_____ It would help my teaching if each classroom had video capability.

_____ It would help my teaching if each academic building had a dedicated AV room.

_____ An AV technology-rich classroom can be a distraction to real learning.

_____ AV technology-rich classrooms pander to a passive learning style, e.g. watching TV.

_____ Learning expectations are so changed in an AV "technology classroom" that they are harmful.

Obstacles to Technology:

_____ I really don't have the time to learn new AV technologies.

_____ I need much more institutional support to get the training I need to use teaching AV technologies.

_____ The learning curve for new AV technologies is usually not worth the trouble.

_____ AV Technology will be distributed unfairly and that will lead to destructive resentment.

_____ I don't know what AV technology is available in my discipline.

_____ I am worried about maintenance of equipment if AV is decentralized.

_____ The economic environment in higher education is not likely to support significant technological advances

Selected Issues:

_____ I would use Science 200A&B for my teaching, if it were properly equipped.

_____ Priority should be given to updating the AV equipment in the large auditoria on campus, e.g. R01, W101.

_____ I already have access to materials without the help of the library.

_____ Technology will likely be implemented piecemeal and inefficiently.

The general question we are asking here is how intensive a user of AV technology have you been and how intensive a user are you likely to be in the future. Indicate both your past and probable future use of each of the following technologies, regardless of whether for teaching or research, used at home or on campus applications. Use a 0 through 9 scale whose endpoints indicate that:

        0 = I have never used or never plan to use this technology

        9 = I have used or probably will use this technology everyday

	Past (0-9)	Future (0-9)		Past (0-9)	Future (0-9)
Videos	____	____	CD-Rom	____	____
Films	____	____	MultiMedia	____	____
Transparencies	____	____	Computers	____	____
Slides	____	____	Other (specify):	____	____
Cassettes	____	____	_____	____	____

Department:_____ School:_____

Years at WPC: _____ Rank (circle one): Inst. Asst. Assoc. Full

Gender: M F Age: _____ Year in which you received highest degree: _____

Return this survey to: AV Department, Library by April 30, 1995
If you would like to see a report of the results of this survey, contact Jane Hutchison at X2980.

Please add any comments which will help us serve you better.

Reports

Eastern Washington University
Results and analysis of a survey on library research skills.

Marist College
An excerpt from an accreditation self-study report which illustrates the analysis of the administration of the materials availability instrument from *Measuring Academic Library Performance*.

Hawaii Pacific University
Analysis of a study done on use of libraries by students in off-campus programs.

FINAL TOTAL
INFORMATION SURVEY
FALL 1993

Please circle or indicate appropriate choice below.

1. How important do you think library research skills are for you to complete coursework in your major successfully?

n=457   6 (1%)   36 (8%)   16 (4%)   216 (47%)   183 (40%)
(100%) unimportant   somewhat unimportant   no opinion   important   very important

2. How important do you feel library research skills are for students at the university in general to complete their courses successfully ?

n=456   1 (0%)   21 (5%)   24 (5%)   261 (57%)   149 (33%)
(100%) unimportant   somewhat unimportant   no opinion   important   very important

3. How important do you feel library research skills are for students in your field to succeed in a job after graduation?

n=457   9 (2%)   64 (14%)   60 (13%)   212 (46%)   112 (25%)
(100%) unimportant   somewhat unimportant   no opinion   important   very important

4. How comfortable do you feel about your own ability to locate library research materials on a topic of your choice?   4-1 n=34 (100%)   10 (29%) no   24 (71%) yes   (see explanation in
                   4-5 n=34 (100%)   21 (62%) no   13 (38%) yes   (commentary below)

n=457   34 (7.5%)   124 (27%)   10 (2%)   255 (56%)   34 (7.5%)
(100%) uncomfortable   somewhat uncomfortable   no opinion   comfortable   very comfortable

5. Circle one adjective in each pair which best describes how you feel about library research:

163 (47%)   187 (53%)   111 (33%) 225 (67%)   160 (42%)   219 (58%)
anxious or confident   bored or interested   confused or knowledgeable
n=350 (not 100%)   n=336 (not 100%)   n=379 (not 100%)

6. How many times have you been assigned a research paper at Eastern? (Choose only one.)

Rank	Percent	n=457 (100%)
1	33%	__153_ at least once a quarter
2	28%	__129_ more than once a quarter
3	26%	__118_ at least once a year
4	8%	___36_ never--new to university
5	5%	___21_ no research papers assigned while at Eastern

7. What kinds of library research assignments have you had at Eastern? (Choose all that apply.)

Rank	Percent	n=457 (not 100% due to multiple responses)
3	42%	__190_ book review
4	33%	__154_ speech
1	76%	__347_ short research paper (3-5 pages)
2	67%	__304_ long research paper (6 pages or more)
5	21%	___98_ statistics information
7	9%	___42_ none, because I am new to the University
6	10%	___47_ other, please specify_____

8.   Who taught you how to use a library: (Choose all that apply.)
Rank Percent   n=457 (not 100% due to multiple and incomplete responses)
   1   64%   __294_on my own
   6   14%   ___65_librarian in a class at EWU
   5   23%   _103_professor of a class
   2   37%   _167_librarian at the reference desk
   4   28%   _129_friend
   3   36%   _164_librarian at high school or public library
   7   14%   __62_librarian in a class at another college
   8   9%   __41_work experience in a library
   9   5%   __22_I do not think that I know how to use the library
   10   4%   __19_other, please specify_____

9.   Do you think library research skills should be taught? When? Please comment below.
n=457 (100%)   407 (89%) yes   23 (5%) no   27 (6%) no response

               n=457 (not 100% due to multiple and incomplete responses)
               24 (5%) k-college   61 (13%) 9-12 61
               32 (7%) k-6   110 (24%) English 101/201
               36 (8%) 7-8   92 (20%) Freshman/transfer

10.   What is your major?_____

11.   Please name an index that would locate journal articles on a topic in your major.
         Guess, if you are not sure.

n=455 (100%)   ____yes 140 (31%) ____   no 252 (55%)_____maybe 63 (14%)_____

12.   Please name a journal in your major. Guess, if you are not sure.

n=455 (100%)   ____yes 289 (64%) ____   no 141 (31%) _____maybe 25 (5%)_____

13.   Which tool in the library can you use to find which books the library owns? Guess, if you are   not
sure.

n=455 (100%)   ____yes 200 (44%) ____   no 130 (29%) _____maybe 125 (27%)_____

14.   Did you transfer to EWU from another school: n=448 (100%)   yes 271 (60%)   no 177 (40%)

         n=443 (100%)   0 (0%)   29 (7.5%)   161 (36%)   193 (43.5%)   60 (13.5%)
15.   Your overall GPA?   below 2.0   2.0-2.6   2.7-3.2   3.3-3.7   above 3.7

            Rank Percent n=453 (100%)   Rank Percent
16.   Are you: 6   0% ___0_freshman   3   14% __63_sophomore
               1   39% _178_junior   2   36% _163_senior
               4   10% __45_post B.A.   5   1% ___4_other

            Rank Percent n=452 (100%)   Rank Percent
17.   Are you: 4   8% __34_17-19   1   44% _200_20-22
               2   20% _91_23-25   6   6% __29_26-28
               7   4% __17_29-31   3   11% __48_31-40
               5   7% __33_40-

COMMENTARY

Methodology

In October 1993 I initially contacted 26 faculty to request participation in the survey. Faculty were selected randomly. First, I identified appropriate courses (300 level) among all courses listed in the Fall 1993 course announcement. Next, I generated random numbers by placing my pen on pages as I flipped through the phone book. I retained the four-digit suffix of the phone number nearest to my pen. For each number, I used the first two digits to select a page in the course announcement and I used the second two digits to identify one of the appropriate courses that I had identified. Through this means, I identifed nearly thirty courses representing nearly all of the majors. Majors not represented by this survey reflect a lack of interest or time by the instructor of the course selected. Some majors, such as music or psychology, had multiple representation.

In November and December I delivered the survey to those faculty who had responded favorably. Due to poor attendance in some of the classes, I expanded my pool of responses by asking several faculty for additional opportunities to reach other classes. I also surveyed a class for which I had provided instruction six weeks before, Bachman's Applied Psychology 403 class. In total, I surveyed 457 students in 18 classes.

Results of the survey

1. Of course, it is heartening that 87% of the respondants thought that library research skills were important to succeed in coursework in their major. One wonders about the 13% who had no opinion or thought that the library was unimportant.

2. An even greater number of respondants (90%) felt library research skills in general are important for students to complete the coursework successfully. As one would expect, in comparing 1 with 2 a smaller number felt that it was very important for general coursework versus coursework in the major. Yet, the positive response to question 2 is greater than question one. What does this suggest? Perhaps some students perceive it to be more important for others than for themselves.

3. Here we see the number of "very important" responses erode as "somewhat unimportant" and "no opinion" rises. The link between library research and job success is less recognized by a greater number; however, the "important" responses do hold steady. A future study that correlated these responses may indicate the cause of this eroded link.

4. First, an explanation is in order. I examined the responses of the 68 students who felt extremely comfortable or uncomfortable. In looking at their responses to the library awareness questions (11-13), I concluded whether or not they should feel that way. Of course, this is just a rough estimation, but it appears that 71% of the "uncomfortable" respondants were justified in feeling uncomfortable and 62% of the "very comfortable" respondants were overestimating their awareness.

In looking at the overall responses to this question, we see a substantial number of negative responses. In the results from some classes, students were evenly split on this question, with equal or even greater number responding in the negative.

5. The responses to this question were inconsistent due to the inability of some to understand the question. Instead of circling one adjective in each pair, some respondants circled one pair or one adjective only. Any conclusions to these responses should be made very carefully. Nonetheless, it appears that an equal numbers are either anxious or confident, that twice as many respondants are interested as compared to those who are bored, and that a modest portion feel more knowledgeable than those who feel confused. When given a choice between confusion and knowledge, a greater portion choose confusion (43%) than the (34.5%) who claim to be uncomfortable. Perhaps the wording or the either/or choice account for this difference. The really

gratifying response is the large portion of "interested" responses. If only two-thirds of the students who came to the information desk were interested in their assignment or research project!

6. This question needs to be reworded--"at least once a quarter" and "more than once a quarter" are really just the same thing! Some of the 5% of the respondants who had not had research paper assignments at Eastern were seniors, but I did not check to see if they were transfers. Given some of the comments (such as "it is a shame that I did not have to write more papers"), this question could be expanded to include several open-ended questions on the perceived importance of research assignments.

7. The ranking indicated the perceived frequency of each of the listed activites. Clearly, short and long research papers are required of the bulk of our students. I wonder how many of the respondants to "statistics information" were looking for an isolated statistic versus those who used statistics in a paper. This raises the question of the perceived utility of government documents as a resource to find statistics or other information. This also raises the question of the perceived use of various collections of the University Libraries--CALS, Government Documents, Special Collections, Curriculum Lab, Sights and Sounds, Periodicals, Music Library, and Reference Collection. Perhaps it would be useful if students checked off the areas of the library that they have used in the past year. This underscores the need to publicize specific collections. For example, none of the 23 students in Kazemek's education class at the Spokane Center knew about the CALS Library just two blocks away. (Many of these students had used the downtown public library, walking right past CALS!) This question could also be improved by modifying "book review" to "book review or article review" since a large number of the "other" responses included article reviews. Several students noted that a 6 page paper is not long!

8. As one would expect, many students teach themselves how to use the library. (I did not note the number of students who responded to this single criterion alone.) It is interesting to note that students have been assisted by friends in nearly the same proportion as a librarian or their professor. It would be interesting to see student rank these sources of assistance (including themselves) in terms of reliability, accuracy, relevance, "approachability", or other criteria. Responses to this question could indicate the degree to which "library anxiety" has been resolved and who is in a favorable position to resolve anxiety. We could also indicate to students that friends are kind, familiar resources that are frequently unreliable. Students could be then shown the value of having a librarian a friend. Perhaps students see librarians in a role of authority to help bail them out at the last minute when a paper is due. Perhaps they see librarians as friends that can help them when they are desperate. On the other hand, librarians may not be seen as friends--this explains the occasional discourtesy when students expect us to bail them out. Of course, these perceptions vary among individuals.

9. This question received a large set of useful responses. Selections from these responses are included below in a separatate section.

Most students felt that library research skills should be taught. Most objections argued that teaching library research skills was unnecessary for the following reasons: a) it was already taught to them at the lower grades, b) that extensive BI was a waste of time, c) that the interaction at the reference desk made extensive BI unnecessary, d) that the library was easy to use, and e) that their instructors (especially in English 101/201) had already covered library research. If their previous experiences in library instruction had been simply tours, then their objections are legitimate in that they have not experienced the benefits of instruction. It is significant that the vast majority were positive about instruction.

Responses to the question "when?" varied from time of day to time in one's educational career. I recorded only those responses that indicated appropriate times in one's education. Respondants most frequently identifed English 101/201 as an appropriate setting. A slightly smaller margin indicated that the Freshman year (or the intial term for transfer students) was an important time for instruction. It is gratifying to note that 5% of the total respondents recognized the constant need for bibliographic instruction throughout one's educational experience.

10. Nearly all majors were represented in this survey.

11-13. Note: Yes indicates a correct answer. No indicates an incorrect or blank answer. Maybe indicates an answer that could possibly be true, but required greater elaboration. For example, many respondants indicated that "the computer" or "the library computer" or "the computer in the reference area" would provide journal citations or indicate library holdings. In these instances, I recorded the response as maybe.

More than half of the respondants could not identify a periodical index in their major. In contrast, nearly two-thirds of the respondants could identify a journal in their major. (In some sessions, I had a few minutes to discuss the survey. I frequently indicated that the library has more than one journal in a person's major and that one way to identify additional journals would be to look on nearby shelves or look in the index area for titles with the same initial letters in the call number. This connection between index and journal title was a surprise to quite a few.) The response that reflected the greatest ambiguity was question 13. One-quarter of the respondants refered to ELIS as "the computer". Guides such as Summary of the electronic resources in JFK Library may help resolve this confusion. Several respondants referred to "librarians" as a tool to identify books.

14. One of the problems in teaching library research skills is the large number of transfer students. Sixty percent of respondants were transfer students. The proposed liberal arts reform may provided the mechanism to reach transfer students.

15. I did not compare grade point average with other components of the survey. The large number (57%) of GPA's above 3.3 may indicate that grade inflation renders any attempt at correlation between GPA and other criteria futile.

16. The survey was successful in reaching the target population. Exactly three-quarters of the respondants were juniors or seniors. No freshman were polled in this survey.

17. The bulk of the respondants were in the 20 to 25 age range. Nonetheless, 28% of all respondants were 26 or older.

Variance among classes by major

Students in psychology courses tended have greater success in identifying indexes, relevant journal titles and the name of the catalog as compared to other majors. In addition, the previously instructed Applied Psychology 403 class responded as expected--indicating to a much greater degree comfort and skill in using the library than the total averages. In the Psychology 403 class, 20 out of 23 identified a journal title in their major. This is 87% success rate (versus the mere 64% of all responses) who could identify a title. It would have been useful to know if their greater skill level were attributable to their previous instruction or related to their class standing (22 out of 23 were seniors). This issue should be addressed by future surveys.

Implication for future surveys

The purpose of this survey was to identify general student attitudes and skills regarding library research. This survey will provide a rich set of general comparative data through yearly measurements of the impact of the instructional program of the University Libraries. My major concern is continuity. I have noted above several changes and addition to make the survey tool a better instrument. How do we improve the instrument, yet maintain continuity? I suggest that we leave questions 1-4, 8, and 10-17 unchanged to maintain this continuity. Questions 5,6,7, and 9 need refinement. Perhaps more open-ended questions on these issues would be helpful.

More complex comparisons among groups were not possible since all surveys were scored by hand. Given the diversity of the respondents and the lack of a control group, I concluded that it was inappropriate to attempt much more than cursory comparisons. Results from the demographic portion of the survey indicate that participants varied in transfer status, GPA, class standing, and age category to a great degree, such that single factors are difficult to identify as causal agents. Future surveys with greater focus may be necessary, especially when combined with personal interviews.

LIBRARY USE AND ASSESSMENT

Student use of the library was studied intensively during the Spring and Fall semesters of 1991. Observation and survey results indicate that most students visit the Library mainly for reading and studying. Only a third of the students in the Library on a typical day during the academic year appear to actually use library materials and resources.

A survey instrument developed by the Ad Hoc Committee on Performance Measures for the Association of College and Research Libraries and adapted for Marist College Library use was used to measure the availability of library materials to students. The results show that 68% of the students responding to the survey were **not** using library materials that day, meaning they were probably studying their own materials or socializing. Results from mid semester show 50% of the students just studying, while after Thanksgiving the percentage jumped higher. The breakdown of library use by class shows the juniors (38%) use the library more than sophomores and seniors (24%) each, with freshman representing only 14% of the undergraduates visiting the Library.

Among the 32% of the students who actively sought library materials during the survey period, the success rate in finding specific materials students actually wanted for their coursework or research needs are as follows:

> 62% success for all periodicals sought
> 72% success for books owned by Marist
> (may or may not be on shelf)
> 84% success for periodicals actually owned by Marist

This result indicates that among students actually seeking library materials they are successful in a majority of the situations. These findings present a sharp contrast to the opinions of students and alumni on their satisfaction with library resources as reported in previous opinion surveys distributed at registration and from Institutional Research. One must ask the question whether these students actually use library materials or rather base their opinion on reputation. As librarians and faculty actively involved in library programs, we know that resources in some areas such as business are very extensive and up-to-date. When students are not satisfied at Marist in 1992 with library resources, considering the extent of collection development that has taken place over the last five years, one must ask the following questions:

- Has the student asked a librarian for help to find materials?
- Has the student participated in a library instruction class?
- Has the faculty member teaching the course participated in collection development in the discipline or adapted the syllabus to library holdings?

Analyzing the survey by major, we found a high correlation between student success in finding library materials and faculty involvement in library programs, such as the approval plan or bibliographic instruction. For example, the students majoring in political science had a 90% success rate finding materials they needed. This is a discipline where all of the faculty teaching full loads are very active in library programs and collection building.

The daily count of library traffic indicates that approximately 7,000 student visit the library occur during a typical week of the semester, with the majority seeking study space as revealed by the survey discussed above. It is apparent that there is not enough quality study space to handle the need.

Student assignments seem to determine active usage of library materials, with little demand for recreational or supplemental reading interests. As noted previously, there are indications that half the course work at the undergraduate level does no require library usage to complete assignments. This obviously leaves a gap in potential demand.

The audiovisual, periodical, reference and general book collections are all heavily used during the semester. The Library circulated over 31,000 books last year. This represents 1/3 of the entire book collection by title.

EXECUTIVE SUMMARY

BACKGROUND

During satellite campus term 4-93, Meader Library distributed the Satellite Campus Student Library Usage Survey to all satellite campus instructors teaching during that term. It was our intention to target the entire student population enrolled in courses during term 4-93, regardless of their academic status.

The purpose of the survey was threefold:

1. To establish a statistical record of satellite campus student library usage patterns.

2. To determine which libraries are being used by satellite campus students.

3. To plan for better and more relevant outreach services to the satellite campus community in accordance with WASC Standards 6.B.2 and 6.D.5.

CONCLUSIONS

1. Of the combined total of 2,875 students enrolled on all military campuses during Term 4-93, 858 completed surveys were returned. This constitutes a return rate of approximately 33.5%.

2. Of the 858 students who returned a completed survey, 125 or 14.6% reported having used Meader Library for their HPU class-related library research needs.

3. 37 or 29.6% of the 125 respondents who reported having used Meader Library for their research needs also cited a number of deficiencies with Meader Library. These included: (1) not enough CD-Rom's, (2) not enough material on Latin America, (3) material is too outdated, (4) not enough current accounting material, (5) not enough serial holdings in computer science area, and (6) annual report collection not extensive enough.

4. Base libraries were noted as being used more often than any other type of library by the satellite campus community for HPU class-related library research needs.

5. Hickam Base Library was noted as the most frequently used of the base libraries.

6. Of the deficiencies reported by 182 or 29.7% of the 430 respondents who reported having used a base library for their research needs, the most often cited included: (1) inadequate serial holdings, (2) material is too outdated, (3) not enough business-related material, and (4) not enough computer-related material.

7. Public libraries were noted as being the second most frequently used type of library by the satellite community.

8. The most often used UH Library System library was Hamilton Library on the UH Manoa Campus. Of the community college libraries, the most often used was Leeward Community College in Pearl City.

9. "Other" libraries reported as having been used by 21 of the 858 total respondents included: Wheeler AAF Library, Aliamanu Military Reservation Library, NCTAMS EastPac Library, and the Hawaii Medical Library.

10. Of the 858 students who completed the survey, 177 or 20.6% provided comments/suggestions on how the HPU Library System might improve outreach services to the satellite campus communities.

11. The most frequently mentioned suggestion on how the HPU Library System might improve outreach services to the satellite campus communities was the need to increase the proliferation of Library System information (to include more advertising and promotion of the resources and services available to satellite campus students).

DETAILED STATISTICS

MEADER LIBRARY

1.   Of the 858 total responses:

    —   39 or 4.5% reported having a student borrower's card.

    —   123 or 14.3% reported having seen the Meader Library Fact Sheet.

    —   149 or 17.4% reported being aware of the hours and services offered by Meader Library.

    —   125 or 14.6% reported having used Meader Library for their HPU class-related library research needs.

    —   Of these 125 who reported having used Meader Library for their HPU class-related library research needs:

        —   112 or 89.6% reported having used Meader Library between 1 and 5 times per term.

        —   10 or 8% reported having used Meader Library more than 5 times per term.

        —   100 or 80% reported having used Meader Library on weekday evenings or on weekends.

        —   24 or 19.2% reported not having used Meader Library on weekday evenings or on weekends. (We can assume that they used Meader Library between 8:00 and 5:00, Monday-Friday).

        —   71 or 23.1% reported having used Meader Library to locate periodical articles; this being the most common reason for using Meader Library.

        —   88 or 70.4% reported having been able to find all the information that they needed in Meader Library.

        —   90 or 72% reported having asked a reference librarian for assistance while at Meader Library.

2.   Of the 858 total responses:

    —   736 or 85.8% reported not being aware of the Meader Library Guide series.

    —   772 or 90% reported that they had never used the PERFAX Service.

    —   47 or 5.5% reported having used the PERFAX Service.

    —   39 or 4.5% had no response.

BASE LIBRARIES

1.   Of the 858 total responses:

    —   612 or 71.3% reported having used a base library for their HPU class-related library research needs.

    —   Of the 612:

2

- 266 or 30.3% reported having used Hickam Base Library for their HPU class-related library research needs. (Hickam Base Library is the most widely used base library as inferred from the statistics).

- 246 or 28% reported having used Sgt. Yano Post Library (Schofield Barracks) for their HPU class-related library research needs.

- 367 or 60% reported having used a base library between 1 and 5 times per term.

- 430 or 70.3% reported having been able to find all the information that they needed.

HAWAII STATE PUBLIC LIBRARIES

1. Of the 858 total responses:

- 447 or 52.1% reported never having used the Hawaii State Public Library System for their HPU class-related library research needs.

- 381 or 44.4% reported that they had used the HSPLS for their HPU class-related library research needs.

- Of the 381:

  - 259 or 68% reported that they did not use their own personal computer and modem to access the databases of the HSPLS.

  - 100 or 26.2% reported having used their own personal computer and modem to access the databases of the HSPLS.

  - 249 or 65.4% reported having used the HSPLS between 1 and 5 times per term.

  - 100 or 26.2% reported having used the HSPLS over 5 times per term.

  - 284 or 74.5% reported having been able to find all the information that they needed.

UNIVERSITY OF HAWAII LIBRARIES

1. Of the 858 total responses:

- 665 or 77.5% reported never having used the UH Library System for their HPU class-related library research needs.

- 148 or 17.2% reported having used the UH Library System for their HPU class-related library research needs.

- Of the 148:

  - 102 or 68.9% reported that they had not used their own personal computer and modem to access the databases of the UH Library System.

  - 42 or 28.4% reported having used their own personal computer and modem to access the databases of the UH Library System.

  - 109 or 73.6% reported having used the UH Library System between 1 and 5 times per term.

3

– 34 or 23% reported having used the UH Library System more than 5 times per term.

– 131 or 88.5% reported having been able to find all the information that they needed.

"OTHER" LIBRARIES

1. Of the 858 total responses:

    – 707 or 82.4% reported that they had never used a library other than those mentioned in the survey for their HPU class-related library research needs.

    – 21 or 2.4% reported that they had used a library other than those mentioned in the survey for their HPU class-related library research needs.

    – Of the 21:

        – 13 or 61.9% reported having been able to find all the information that they needed.

        – 7 or 33.3% had no response.

COMMENTS/SUGGESTIONS MADE BY STUDENTS

(in order of precedence)

1. Proliferate more information on resources and services available to satellite campus students.
2. Provide dial-in access to HPU Library System collection (including CD-ROM access).
3. Need for improved and more parking in the downtown campus area.
4. Provide for ID card processing on satellite campuses during registration period.
5. Need for more CD-ROM products in HPU Libraries (particularly in the computer science areas).
6. Need for a new student orientation on satellite campuses each term.
7. Need for greater depth at the graduate level in the Meader Library collection (particularly in the areas of math, business, and law).
8. Need to establish resource-sharing network between HPU Library System and base libraries.
9. Need to inform satellite campus counselors of library resources and services available to students.
10. HPU Libraries are too far away to be convenient.
11. Need to establish ILL services between HPU Libraries and satellite campus offices.
12. Need to inform satellite campus instructors of library resources and services available to students.
13. Need to establish access to the Internet.
14. Need to provide modem access to HPU Library System through HPU Computer Center terminals on military sites.
15. Need to open up access to base libraries for all satellite campus students.
16. Need to allow for faxing of information to any fax machine.
17. Need to establish HPU "satellite libraries" on all military campuses.
18. Need to arrange for satellite campus student HPU library tours.
19. Need to subsidize bus passes for satellite campus students.
20. Need to provide a shuttle service between base sites and the HPU Libraries (since there is already a shuttle service between the downtown and Hawaii Loa campuses).
21. Need to offer a class on how to use a library.

4

Accompanying Documents

Sweet Briar College
Philadelphia College of Pharmacy and Science
> Survey researchers feel that a good cover letter included with a mailed survey increases the response rate. Two examples.

Transylvania University
> Instructions for those distributing a survey in a library. Again, a very important influence on response rate.

Gardner-Webb University
> A reward, or chance of a reward, has also been shown to increase response rate. An example of providing both.

Concordia College
> An easy and imaginative follow-up and to increase responses.

Monday, April 6, 1992

Dear Library Assistant,

The library is assessing the need for future library facilities to serve Sweet Briar. Please help by completing the attached survey. Your participation is critical because a high percentage of returned surveys will provide a reliable and comprehensive review of perceptions and recommendations. As one of the most knowledgeable groups in the Sweet Briar Community about library matters, your input is most important

Please take a few minutes over the next few days to complete the questionnaire. A pretest indicates that completion should take approximately ten to fifteen minutes. A return envelope is enclosed for your convenience. Space is provided at the end of the questionnaire for additional comments. Please take advantage of that opportunity to expand on your views. Responses will be completely confidential and results will be reported in the aggregate.

At present we are making certain assumptions in our planning. These include the desire to retain the current site of the Mary Helen Cochran library as the site for Sweet Briar's main library facility. We assume the current and future uses populations will remain essentially similar and stable. This means our planning is based on approximately 100 faculty members, 300 staff members and 650 students. In addition, there are between 350 and 500 other users, comprised of Friends of the Library, VCCA fellows, high school students enrolled in honors courses at the local high school and at Sweet Briar and miscellaneous other users.

We also assume the continuing consortial relationship with Randolph-Macon Woman's College and Lynchburg College, use of computer resources and non-traditional mechanisms of information distribution in conjunction with printed books and journals and interlibrary loan and the increased use of other technologies such as satellite and television. Finally, we believe research will become increasingly interdisciplinary, as it has over the past decade, and will make increasingly intensive use of new technologies.

Please return the completed questionnaire to me. Thanking you sincerely for your help in this planning, I remain,

Sincerely yours,

John G. Jaffe
Director of Libraries and
Media Services

FROM: Mignon Adams
             Director of Library Services

RE: ACPE Accreditation

DATE: March 23, 1995

The ACPE Self-Study Guide for Accreditation asks, "what is the faculty evaluation of services provided by the library?"

In order to answer this question, the attached survey has been developed. It should take no more than ten minutes to answer, and your responses will be important in the accreditation visit.

I would very much appreciate your response by April 10. Those who return the survey by that time may choose to be in a drawing for a carrot cake from The Carrot Cake Man.

- -

Yes! I've completed the survey and I'd like to have my name in a drawing for a wonderful carrot cake from The Carrot Cake Man.

Name_____

Phone_____

(You may return this slip in a different envelope from the survey to: M. Adams, Box 119.)

GUIDELINES/INSTRUCTIONS FOR SURVEYORS

1. Please distribute the General Satisfaction Survey to every person <u>leaving</u> the library. The Materials Availability Survey should be distributed to everyone <u>entering</u> the library but collected as they leave. If someone indicates that he/she wants to bring the survey back at a later time, please say "Thank you, but we really need for you to return the form before you leave today. Perhaps we can catch you at a more convenient time."

2. Be assertive, pleasant, friendly. SMILE.

3. Explain to people that we need <u>their</u> response. Let your manner and willingness to respond to questions convince people of the importance of the survey - this is just as effective as saying "This is really important."

4. The opening line is crucial. Keep it simple and short, but interesting enough to get people's attention. Stress the brevity of the survey form and that the library is doing the survey to improve service in the library.

5. Explain that the survey is intended to measure only <u>today's</u> visit to the library.

6. Use language that is comfortable to you.

7. Answer any questions about the survey form as best you can, but be careful not to influence people's answers (especially on questions that ask for their opinions).

8. If people want to discuss the survey or the library, cooperate within limits; remember, you are here to dispense questionnaires. If they want to complain about or praise the library, encourage them to do so in writing on the back of the survey form.

9. Always tell people how much their input is appreciated, and thank them for filling out a survey form.

10. Remind people to place their survey forms in the collection box.

POSSIBLE OPENING LINES

We'd like to know how satisfied you were with your visit to the library today. Will you help us by filling out this brief survey?

We're doing a survey to assess whether the library is meeting your needs and want your input on today's visit. Would you mind filling this out?

We'd like your help wih our library satisfaction survey. Will you let us know about today's visit by filling out this brief survey?

LINES TO USE IF PEOPLE TRY TO WALK AWAY

Here's a pencil! This will only take a couple of minutes.

We'll use this information to improve our service.

YOUR input is really valuable to us.

If they respond really negatively or positively:

Thanks. We really need to know that. Would you mind writing that in the space for comments?

Once they take a survey, say:

Please place it in the box when you're finished.
We REALLY appreciate your assistance.
Thanks.
You've really been helpful.

And remember to be friendly and smile a lot!

Gardner-Webb University

DO NOT DETACH THIS SHEET FROM QUESTIONNAIRE

Student Name_____

Student ID Number_____

_____

DEADLINE: FRIDAY, JANUARY 20TH !!!!

You must turn in your completed questionnaire directly to the Reference Desk or Mrs. Carolyn Hunt's desk in the Library, or mail to Campus Box 326. Questionnaires received after January 20th will be considered valid responses for the survey, but will not be eligible for 25/35 transaction card copies or prize drawings (see below).

◆ ◆

Complete the questionnaire (all questions answered, comments optional) and receive a new transaction card with **25** copies programmed in. This card will work in our paper and microform copiers. Any student who already has a transaction card may instead have **35** copies added to it.

Also, names will be drawn from among eligible responders for the following prizes:

1.   Lunch for 3 at Uptown Cafe **or** Credit of $25 at the Campus Shop

2.   Dinner for 2 at Satterfields **or** Credit of $40 at the Campus Shop

◆ ◆

DO NOT DETACH THIS SHEET FROM QUESTIONNAIRE

Once we verify the name and ID number for current returning student status and scan the questionnaire to see if all questions have been answered we will detach this sheet to protect the anonymity of your responses. We will prepare a list of students eligible for transaction card copies, then put the top part of this sheet with everyone else's for the prize drawings. If you do win a prize you will be notified and as applicable given a choice of the meal or Campus Shop credit.

4 April 1995

Hi!

About two weeks ago you received a copy of this survey in your mailbox. According to my records your survey number was not returned.

I realize this is a very busy time for students and so I am resorting to bribery (smile). In the time it will take you to unwrap this piece of gum and chew it you can also fill in the questionnaire! Please take a few quick minutes to answer the questions and drop the survey in campus mail. I am really interested in your perceptions of the library and this research can be a part of improving our services to you.

Thank-you for being part of this important project.

(Note: Original had actual piece
of gum attached)